FOUNDATIONS FOR LI

BOO

LEADER'S MANUAL

WITH HELPS AND ANSWERS

This Is My New Life

The way to God and the privileges and opportunities in His Kingdom

by

Dick J. Driedger

Library and Archives Canada Cataloguing in Publication
Driedger, Dick J., 1930-
This is my new life : book one, leader's manual : discover the way to God and the privileges and opportunities in His kingdom / by Dick J. Driedger.
First manual in the Foundations for Living Discipleship Series.
ISBN 978-1-926947-65-5

1. Christian life. I. Foundations for Living Society II. Title.
III. Series: Foundations for Living (Langley, B.C.) bk. 1

BV4511.D75 2009 248.4 C2009-903332-1

THIS IS MY NEW LIFE
Leader's Manual

Copyright © 2020 by Foundations for Living Society. All rights reserved. No portion of this book may be reproduced, stored in a retrieval system, or transmitted in any form or by any means – electronic, mechanical, photocopy, recording, or any other – except for brief quotations in printed reviews, without the prior permission of the publisher.

Unless otherwise indicated, Scripture quotations used in this book are from The Holy Bible, New International Version® (NIV)®. Copyright © 1973, 1978, 1984 International Bible Society. Used by permission of Zondervan Bible Publishers.

Published by
Foundations for Living Society
Surrey, British Columbia, Canada

This Is My New Life/Dick J. Driedger
ISBN 978-1-926947-65-5

1. The Kingdom of Darkness vs. The Kingdom of Light. 2. Entering into the Kingdom of Light. 3. Responsibilities and Growing in the New Kingdom. 4. The Role of the Holy Spirit in maturing the Citizen in the New Kingdom. 5. The Power of the Word of God and Prayer.

Knowing God, His truths, and His principles, is relevant for today's society and will add deeper meaning, purpose and direction to our life. The Foundations for Living logo symbolizes this in three ways:

The ascending steps at the bottom of the figure characterizes the gradual stages of biblical learning that takes place during classes; a process by which to strengthen our faith and lay down a solid foundation for living for God. **(2 Timothy 3:16-17; Romans 15:4; Psalm 119:105)**

The stylized structure resting upon these steps depicts the sturdy home, heart or body that houses our faith when built on the basis of trust, knowledge and deep assurance in our Savior, Jesus Christ. It also stands for the historic Christian church, temple or tabernacle whose door or gateway is always freely open to any who choose to enter. The roof peak reminds us that our focus is ever upwards and continually challenges us to live by our Lord's highest standards. **(Matthew 7:24-26; 16:18; Psalm 31:1-3)**

The sun represents the Son of Righteousness or His crown of glory. God's love shines on us all and by His grace, He grants us hope and peace. When we are committed, faithful and obedient to Him, He promises us growth, wholeness and eternal life. **(John 3:16; 1 Timothy 4:10; Psalm 119:165; 2 Peter 3:18)**

Dedication and Acknowledgments

The Foundations for Living Discipleship Series is dedicated to my wife, Susan, a loving devoted partner whose life has inspired and encouraged me to write this series to disciple numerous new Christians that have been part of our ministry for many years. She has tested the manuals in discipling hundreds of new believers. In the process she has trained many to become disciple-makers and leaders in their church and community.

This discipleship series also owes its development to the hundreds of disciples who have challenged us to refine the material to make it user-friendly for leaders.

Our greatest reward in writing this material is seeing lives changed as students and leaders have researched the Scriptures, and in so doing, found help and hope for Christ-like living.

TABLE OF CONTENTS

FOUNDATIONS FOR LIVING DISCIPLESHIP SERIES

Book One: ***This Is My New Life***

Introduces the student to the Christian faith. It is designed for those who are searching or have just received Jesus Christ as their Savior. It is also an excellent tool to learn how to lead someone to Christ.

Book Two: ***This is My God***

Here is a must for every Christian. A study of the unchanging truths for discernment and godly living. Discover the nature and character of God to help you identify false teachings such as evolution, reincarnation, etc.

Book Three: ***This Is My Freedom***

The focus of this manual is to equip the believer to live a life of victory. You will cover subjects such as: God's role in victory; Satan's role in hindering God's plan for your life; overcoming the power of addictions, anger, and bitterness, etc.

Book Four: ***This Is My Wholeness***

A study designed to take the student through the step-by-step process from the time before he became a Christian, to living an abundant Christian life in the power of the Holy Spirit. The student will trace the journey of the Israelites from Egypt through the Red Sea, to the Desert Wilderness, and through the Jordan River to the Promised Land of Canaan.

For inquiries or orders for all manuals and books,

please email **info@foundations4living.ca**

or visit our website at **www.foundations4living.ca**

PREFACE

A number of aspects of this course make it unique:

1. **The method of study is transferable.** The leader is trained to *lead*, not teach. The motto of every leader is: *"teaching by asking, learning by searching, and growing by obeying."* The art of asking significant questions can change the course of an individual's life. This method of leadership makes the study transferable. The student is encouraged to follow this example when there is opportunity to lead a class.
2. **Its simplicity.** For the Church to become involved in evangelism and discipleship, the vocabulary and terminology must be understood. Where more difficult concepts are explored, they are explained in words the average church member can understand.
3. **Application is key.** Unless a truth discovered is translated into action it has not been learned. In each lesson the student is encouraged to apply the truths learned in order to effect spiritual change.
4. **Its underlying motivation.** The art of making disciples has been all but lost in many of our churches today. This series of courses is designed to help restore the Church to make disciples as mandated by the Great Commission. (Matthew 28: 18-20)
5. **Mobilizing the Church.** The simplicity of the course and the method of leadership makes this an excellent opportunity to get maximum participation by the average church member.
6. **Graded in order of difficulty.** The author has undertaken to lay out this series in order of difficulty, beginning with the easier understood course and progressing to more difficult theological concepts.
7. **A Leader's Manual with helps and suggested answers for every book.** This makes it possible for "nonprofessionals" to be involved in the discipleship ministry. The manual is identical to the Student's Manual except for helps and extra questions interspersed among the questions, and suggested answers in the back.

In all of the classes, the objective is always to effect positive spiritual change in the participant's life.

SOME FEATURES OF THIS MANUAL

THERE ARE FEATURES TO THIS SECOND EDITION THAT SHOULD PROVE HELPFUL TO EACH LEADER

1. It is designed to train leaders to train other leaders as they go through this course.
2. The suggested answers to questions in the Student's Manual are in a separate section (Answer Key) in the back of this manual.
3. Leader's Comments are two types: **T** is for **tips and helps** for the leader (not to be said to the students) and look like this:

T At this point you will simply guide the students through the procedures...

4. **S** is for the leader to **say to the students** and are enclosed in quotation marks:

S "In this class you may feel free to ask questions or express your opinion..."

5. It will be very important for the leader to do his or her work just like the student does. It is well known that the Holy Spirit speaks to each one in a unique way. The answers are there simply to help the leader to cover the concepts for which this course is designed.
6. Note that **page numbers** in the Leader's Manual will not correspond with the Student's Manual, but the **section numbers** will be identical in both manuals.

BEFORE YOU LEAD, FAMILIARIZE YOURSELF WITH THE PURPOSES OF *THIS IS MY NEW LIFE*

1. It is designed for new or pre-Christians.
2. For new or mature Christians to learn how to write and use their testimony, how to share their faith, and how to disciple others using the Foundations for Living Discipleship Series. This first book is a must for everyone leading the courses.

INTRODUCTION

This is My New Life, the first manual in the Foundations for Living Discipleship Series, is specifically designed to mobilize the local church to become disciple-makers as mandated in the Great Commission, and as demonstrated by the early Church (Acts 2:42). Through practical application of the truths discovered, both leaders and students will learn to develop their own testimonies and use them to lead others to the saving knowledge of Jesus Christ.

There is much confusion in Christendom today as to what a Christian is. This first course seeks to clarify what it means to be a Christian. Through research in the Scriptures, leaders and students will contrast the characteristics of the Kingdom of Darkness with the Kingdom of Light. The final goal of this course will then be to illustrate what the Scriptures say about entering into the Kingdom of Light, and how to live victoriously in this Kingdom as a Christian (Christ-follower).

Participants will soon discover this course is not only for those wishing to explore the Christian faith, or for new Christians. Mature Christians will experience growth through interaction and self-discovery of biblical truths. Each lesson will challenge the students to apply what they have learned through searching the Scriptures.

Dick J. Driedger

NOW EXPERIENCE THE THRILL OF
BECOMING A DISCIPLE OF JESUS!

INTRODUCTORY LESSON

BEGINNING AN EXCITING ADVENTURE: THIS IS MY NEW LIFE

I. THIS COURSE IS ALL ABOUT LIFE—*NEW LIFE*

If you are like many of us today, you will probably have asked yourself questions such as, *Who am I? What am I here for? Is there a God? If there is a God, how can I know Him?* And you came up with no answers. Life has become meaningless, and something inside tells you that something is wrong, but you do not know what. You try to fix the inside, but you discover that it doesn't work. What other questions have you been asking? Write them down below:

____

____

____

____

S "In this class you may feel free to ask any questions or express how you feel. You will discover that all of us are still on a journey to find answers."

II. YOU MAY HAVE PURSUED MANY PATHS THAT LEAD TO DEAD ENDS

We often pursue many paths hoping for a solution to the struggle within. Religion may have been one of your pursuits, but to no avail. You may wish to discuss what other paths you have pursued to find a solution to your personal inner struggle.

T It would be appropriate for you to share, if you so desire, to relate some paths that you have searched in the past. Do not, at this point, tell how you found the right path. That will come later.

A. This course is designed to help you settle that struggle within.

In this class you will discover that you have been living in a kingdom for which you have not been created. Everything in this kingdom is designed to destroy you. The kingdom ruler under whose domination you have been living is none other than the Destroyer, Satan. This course is designed to point you to a **New Life** under the **New Citizenship** in the **Kingdom of God.** It is only when you enter this **New Kingdom** you will discover that life will work for you. You were designed to live for God. The laws in **God's Kingdom** will take you to a new dimension of life beyond which you have never even dreamed. At the end of this lesson you will review a chart that will seek to explain the **Two Kingdoms** mentioned above.

T At this point you will simply guide the students through the procedures for going through each lesson. There will be questions which you will seek to answer.

B. Your leader will guide you through this course.

The Foundations for Living Discipleship Series is built on the method known as: **Teach by Asking**, **Learn by Searching**, and **Grow By Obeying.**

1. **TEACH BY ASKING:** How will this work?
   a. The leader will **ask** one person to read the question and the Scripture reference and his answer. (Be sure you wait until each one has found the Scripture before reading the Bible reference.)
   b. After you have given your answer, the leader may **ask** others if they can add any more to what you have given.
   c. Your leader, from time to time, will **ask** you how you could apply the truth you have just learned from the Scriptures. The most frequent missing ingredient in most Bible teaching is **application.**
2. **LEARN BY SEARCHING:** This will be an important and exciting step for you!
   a. You will discover Bible truths as you search the Scriptures on your own. God often speaks to you personally, according to what you need at that time.
   b. To shed more light on a certain subject or truth, your leader may **ask** you to consider and **search** out other Scriptures.
3. **GROW BY OBEYING:** Here is where theory is put into practical test. This is where you **apply** the truth you have learned.

   This study will seek to help you understand the principles of Scripture and encourage you to **obey** what you learn. Scripture becomes practical and leads to growth and maturity only as it is applied to life through **obedience.**

   Let us consider these steps:

a. **Lay a Foundation:** You must have a solid foundation upon which to build. To discover what or who that foundation is, will be one of the pursuits of this class.

b. **Learn:** You will learn and understand the topic by searching God's Word, the Bible, and getting the meaning on your own. You will get the most out of each lesson when you do it before you come to class. The Bible encourages the study of the Word on your own. Read Acts 17:11.

S "Here is your first opportunity to use the Bible in this class. We will all wait to help you find the passage before we begin to read it. Then assign I will someone to read that passage and give the answer."

What do the Scriptures call the people who search the Scriptures to find out on their own that the things being taught are, indeed, true?

___

c. **Obey:** When you understand a principle and act upon it, your obedience will lead you to the next level of growth. The Bible teaches that growing as a Christian is like building a house. Let's look at this example from the first book in the New Testament in Matthew 7:24-27.

i. What was the positive aspect of obeying what you hear?

___

___

ii. What did you see as the result of not obeying what you hear?

___

___

S "Is there someone here who may wish to share a 'storm' you experienced, that had it not been for God helping you, it would have been disastrous in your life?"

T Allow a few minutes, just to give opportunity for someone to share if they sense a need to do so.

iii. You probably came to the conclusion that obedience to the Word of God builds a foundation to help weather the storms that life hands us. In the lessons to come, you will have an opportunity to build the foundation and then build upon that foundation through obedience.

C. The Two Spiritual Kingdoms Contrasted

You will now consider the goal of this course: **to search the Word of God for the key to transferring your citizenship from the Kingdom of Darkness to the Kingdom of Light.** Together with your leader, consider the page entitled, "The Two Spiritual Kingdoms Contrasted". The goal of this chart is to illustrate the difference between the Kingdom of Darkness and the Kingdom of Light. The rest of the course will help you discover how you can **transfer your citizenship** from the Kingdom of Darkness to the Kingdom of Light.

Let us now begin this course and the exciting adventure of becoming part of a "noble-minded generation" (Acts 17:11) as we start the process of **teaching by asking, learning by searching and growing by obeying.**

S "Let's look at the chart on the next page to discover the characteristics of the Two Spiritual Kingdoms. We will not be able to discuss how we can get from the Kingdom of Darkness to the Kingdom of Light; that will be for a later lesson. In fact, that is one of the major goals of this class."

THE TWO SPIRITUAL KINGDOMS CONTRASTED

"...giving thanks to the Father who has qualified you to share in the inheritance of the saints in the kingdom of light. For He has rescued us out of the dominion of darkness and brought us into the kingdom of the Son he loves in whom we have redemption, the forgiveness of sins." Colossians 1:12-14

KINGDOM OF DARKNESS RULED BY SATAN

- **We all enter the Kingdom of Darkness by natural birth (we are imperfect sinners at birth).**
  Psalm 51:5 *Surely I was sinful at birth, sinful from the time my mother conceived me.*

- **God did not create us for this Kingdom.**
  1 Thessalonians 5:5 *We do not belong to the night or to the darkness.*

- **The ruler of this Kingdom is Satan (our enemy)**
  1 Peter 5:8 *Your enemy, the devil, prowls around like a roaring lion looking for someone to devour.*

- **After death, people in this Kingdom will experience Hell (total separation from God).**
  2 Thessalonians 1:8-9 *He (God) will punish those who do not know God and do not obey the gospel of our Lord Jesus. They will be punished with everlasting destruction and shut out from the presence of the Lord and from the majesty of His power.*

KINGDOM OF LIGHT RULED BY GOD

- **God made a way for us to receive new citizenship in His Kingdom.**
  John 3:3 *...no one can enter the kingdom of God unless he is born again.*

- **Only in this kingdom will life work for us.**
  Matthew 6:33 *But seek first His Kingdom and His righteousness, and all these things will be given to you.*

- **Jesus gives us power to change.**
  2 Peter 1:3 *His divine power has given us everything we need for life and godliness...*

- **The laws and privileges in God's Kingdom through Jesus Christ will take us into a new dimension in life.**
  2 Corinthians 5:17 *...if anyone is in Christ, he is a new creation; the old has gone, the new has come.*

- **After death, people in this Kingdom will experience Heaven (living with God)**
  2 Corinthians 5:1 *Now we know if the earthly tent we live in is destroyed we have a building from God, an eternal house in heaven, not built by human hands.*

LESSON 1

FACING LIFE AS IT REALLY IS

INTRODUCTION

For most of us, life is not what we thought it would be. Our youthful minds painted many pictures that did not include the problems, sufferings, temptations, struggles, despair, and toil which are part of life for most of us. This lesson will help us to assess where our life has been, where we are now, and where, by following God's design for us, we can make a new beginning and live a life of satisfaction and purpose. The reconstruction begins when God comes into the picture. He knows us and longs to have fellowship with us. When we respond to Him with sincerity of heart, He will give us renewed hope as we follow the steps to renewal as He has designed in His Word, the Bible.

> **T** After the reading of this section you may wish to ask questions like: "How has life been different from what you expected?" OR you may wish to say, "It is good to remember that there is always a new beginning with God." This would give hope to someone who may at this time be living in despair.

KEY VERSES

> **S** "For this first lesson you will not need to turn to many verses in your Bible. They are printed here for us, to make it somewhat easier. As I read these Bible verses, underline what you consider to be the key thoughts."

Ecclesiastes 3:9-14 *[9]What does the worker gain from his toil? [10]I have seen the
burden God has laid on men. [11]He has made everything beautiful in its time. He
has also set eternity in the hearts of men; yet they cannot fathom what God has
done from beginning to end. [12]I know that there is nothing better for men than
to be happy and do good while they live. [13]That everyone may eat and drink, and
find satisfaction in all his toil—this is the gift of God. [14]I know that everything
God does will endure forever; nothing can be added to it and nothing taken from
it. God does it so that men will revere him.* *

> **S** "Expressing our feelings and our thoughts often helps to analyze our lives so that we can make meaningful, lasting, and positive adjustments. In the next section of this lesson you will have opportunity to discover the reason or meaning of your feelings and thoughts. Feel free to share these with the group if you sense they might be helpful to all of us."

*All Scripture quotations are from the New International Version © Zondervan Bible Publishers

I. FACING THE REALITY OF MY LIFE

A. Life as I Feel and See It

1. Ecclesiastes 3:9-10 describes life as a burden and toil. What are the aspects of life that you find to be a burden and toil (work or effort that exhausts the body or mind)?

____

____

____

____

T It will be important for you to seek to create a relaxed atmosphere where your group will feel free to share what they find difficult in life. This will vary from person to person. Allow them freedom to share what they find difficult in life. Make mental notes that will help you assess where your students are spiritually and emotionally. You might want to lead off by sharing what you find a burden in life.

The section below will help you further in seeking to assess where your students are. Encourage your students to share any items covered in #2.

2. When life hands you more than you believe you can bear, you feel you need to be able to shed it somewhere to get relief. The items below are intended to help you take an inventory of your life. Put a check in the column that applies to you. If the statement to the right is real put a check under, **Is Real**. If it is not real and you would like it to be real, put a check under the column, **I Would Like to:**

Is Real	I Would Like to:	
☐	☐	discover the meaning and purpose of life.
☐	☐	have a new start and leave my past behind.
☐	☐	receive forgiveness of my past.
☐	☐	leave behind my bitterness and hatred.
☐	☐	have peace in my heart.
☐	☐	have my finances turned around and my debts paid.
☐	☐	know for sure I will go to heaven when I die.

Is Real	I Would Like to:	
☐	☐	be free from the guilt of my past.
☐	☐	be free from the torment of the devil.
☐	☐	know what to do with the burdens of life that are upon me.
☐	☐	know for certain there is a God.
☐	☐	get rid of my fears of death, accidents, etc.
☐	☐	see peace among my family members.
☐	☐	know all my sins are forgiven.
☐	☐	know how to deal with my problems.
☐	☐	have a place where I know I can share and leave my burdens.
☐	☐	be freed from my substance abuse addictions.

You may wish to list some other fears. Write them in the space below:

____

____

____

S "Does anyone wish to share from one of the points in the section above?"

B. Facing the Fact that I Am a Worshiper

All humans are worshipers; therefore our souls finds no rest until God fills that need. (v. 11) A great scientist of the past, Blaise Pascal (1623-1662), once said, "There is a God-shaped vacuum in every person which only God can fill."

1. How would you explain to someone the meaning of this portion of verse 11, "He has also set eternity in the hearts of men"?

____

____

____

S "Every culture, no matter how primitive, has a compulsion to worship. Augustine of ancient times said, 'God made us for Himself, and our heart will be restless until it finds its rest in God.'"

2. What do you believe happens to our souls after our physical death?

____

____

____

T Be prepared for answers such as "I could come back to this earth in another form." "I don't believe there is anything beyond the grave." At this point you are not looking for correct answers, but assessing where your students are. Try not to correct their thinking here. Again, you will make a mental note as to where the students are in their spiritual journey.

S "The question of where our souls go after our physical death is important. Human beings are made up of a mortal body (subject to death), an immortal or undying soul, and an immortal human spirit (the part of our being that perceives the spiritual realm and connects with God). See 1 Thessalonians 5:23; Genesis 2:7. When the body dies, the soul and the spirit of the person leaves the body, and depending on their relationship with Jesus Christ, they either spend eternity with God or apart from Him."

3. Since this search for God is in everyone, different sects, cults, and religions have emerged throughout history. What does verse 11 say about our inability to find the true way?

____

____

____

4. Many people say, "I have my own private faith which will lead me to God". What does the Bible have to say about this? (Proverbs 14:12 or 16:25)

____

____

____

C. God's Intended Life for Me

1. From Ecclesiastes 3:12-13, what did God want our lives to be like?

____

____

T It may be appropriate to share Matthew 6:25-34 to further illustrate God's care for us.

2. What is the origin of this kind of life? (v. 13)

____

____

3. Based on what is revealed in v. 14, what is the implied quality and purpose of God's work?

____

____

II. THE WAY TO HEAVEN AS I UNDERSTAND IT

S "You will notice that none of the statements below qualify us for heaven; however, this information will be very helpful to you in helping this person to receive eternal life in Jesus."

Mark with a check mark what you consider to be the qualifications for heaven:

- ☐ I have had a spiritual experience.
- ☐ When I pray I have a warm feeling.
- ☐ When I am alone in nature I feel God in everything.
- ☐ I am sincere, so it is not so important to God what I believe.
- ☐ I'm a member of a church.
- ☐ I can trust in works of my own.
- ☐ I have been baptized.
- ☐ I have had an out of body experience.
- ☐ I have a "spirit guide" who is my friend.
- ☐ I pray to God every day.

- [ ] I read my Bible.
- [ ] I have always believed in God.
- [ ] I'm thought of as a religious person.
- [ ] I have tried to live a good life.
- [ ] I go to church.
- [ ] I haven't done anything really bad.
- [ ] I have friends who will vouch for me.
- [ ] None of the above
- [ ] ______________________________

At this stage, you were simply asked to indicate what you **understood** to be the qualifications. In the next lesson, we will seek to show what the Bible says about qualifying to receive New Life, or to change our citizenship from the Kingdom of Darkness to the Kingdom of Light.

S "Up to this point you may be saying, 'I am having more questions than answers.' Hopefully, in the next lesson you will get some questions answered that you have been looking for."

LESSON 2

FACING MY SPIRITUAL CONDITION AS GOD SEES IT

T In today's lesson, as in most subsequent lessons, keep in mind that the concepts taught in the Scriptures are contrary to many of society's teachings. Embracing biblical concepts will surely bring conflict as a disciple encounters and experiences the clash between biblical and unbiblical world views.

INTRODUCTION

In this lesson we will not seek to prove that God, heaven, or hell exist. Neither will we seek to prove that the Bible is the only true message of God. These topics will be available in other studies, and to some extent in the lessons to follow. The intent of this lesson is simply to discover what the Bible has to say on the subject of God's intended design for man at creation, and man's fall from that perfect state that was his at creation.

T The Introduction above seeks to avoid a debate or argument as to the truth of concepts that will be discussed. The Bible will speak for itself.

KEY VERSES

S "Underline what you consider to be the main thoughts in the following Scripture verses."

Isaiah 64:6 *All of us have become like one who is unclean, and our righteous acts are like filthy rags; we all shrivel up like a leaf, and like the wind our sins sweep us away.*

1 John 1:8 *If we claim to be without sin, we deceive ourselves and the truth is not in us.*

I. HUMANITY AS ORIGINALLY CREATED BY GOD

The human race has not always been as the two Scriptures above describe. Let us discover what the Bible says about us as we were originally created.

A. God's Purpose in Creating Us

1. Why did God create people according to Genesis 1:26?

S "How is this teaching contrary to our environmentalist teaching today? Today, animals have more rights than people in certain countries."

2. What further things has Psalm 8 to say about the purpose for which God created us?

____

____

S "How is God's honor in humanity contrary to evolutionist teaching? Evolutionists believe that we are just animals coming from a common ancestor, the apes."

3. What do you believe is God's purpose for your life?

____

____

S "What is the pervading thought in our humanistic society today? **It's everyone for himself.** Is it any wonder we are morally, spiritually, and physically wanting in wholeness!"

B. Our Original Condition When God Created Us

1. What did God see to be the condition of Adam (Hebrew *adam* means "man") at the time of his creation? (Genesis 1:31)

____

____

2. Who were we made to be like, and in what aspects do we still mirror that image? Think of capacities that we have that are God-like. (Genesis 1:27)

____

____

S "Why is the question above important?"

T Answer: Because we have a spirit, we have the ability to communicate with God. It is our human spirit that is God-conscious.

You will see from Genesis 1:4, 9 and 12 that everything that God originally created was good.

II. OUR FALL FROM OUR ORIGINAL STATE

T The purpose of this section is to point out the state of the fallenness of our creation when mankind fell through Adam's disobedience, but it will not be a detailed study of God's solution for fallen humanity.

A. How We Fell (Through Adam's Disobedience)

S "This next section will demonstrate that our sin cannot be blamed on environment and heredity. The environment was perfect."

The story of the fall of mankind from God's favor into a life of degradation and self-destruction is described in Genesis 3. Read this account and answer the following questions:

1. What was Satan's first trap to get Eve's attention? (v. 1)

____

S "In what ways do you suppose we are tempted to question God and His purpose for our life?"

2. Once Satan had Eve's attention and interest, what was his next step in having Eve believe him? (v. 5; see also Genesis 2:9)

____

____

S "What questions do we often have about God that cause or tempt us to question His motives for us?"

3. After Eve believed Satan's lie in verse 5, what three steps downward led her to eat of the fruit? (v.6)

____

____

____

S "How does dwelling on and looking at what God has forbidden given rise to yielding to temptation? The battle is often lost with the first look."

4. What are the downward steps to sin as we find it described in James 1:13-15?

____

____

____

5. a. According to James 1:13-15, what responsibility does God put on us when we sin?

____

____

S "What are the spiritual, moral, and physical results of not taking responsibility for our own sins?"

b. Who is really the only one to blame when we fall into sin?

____

____

Note: It is clear from Scripture that unless we acknowledge our sinful condition and are willing to take responsibility for our sin there is no remedy for that sin. This is a necessary concept to keep in mind as we progress through these lessons.

B. The Result of Adam and Eve's Fall

Continue to study Genesis 3 and seek to answer the following questions:

1. Try to interpret from the following Scriptures what new destructive traits Adam and Eve acquired through their disobedience to God.

a) v. 7 ____________________ b) v. 8 ____________________

S **a)** "The result is the emergence of various belief systems. We seek to eliminate guilt without eliminating the cause. A band-aid does not cure a cancer."
b) "How do we try to hide from God? We use alcohol, drugs and such, or avoid other believers."

c) v. 9,10 ______________ d) v. 12,13 ______________

S c) "How do we display our fear of God's presence?"

d) "This is a key in our society. Counsellors and psychiatrists teach this."

Note: You may wish to discuss how these same traits are in all of us today.

2. God pronounced judgment on the serpent (Satan), Adam and Eve.

   a. What judgments did He pronounce upon Eve? (v. 16)

   ____

   ____

   b. List the judgments on Satan, Adam, and Eve as described in verses 17-19.

   ____

   ____

S "What were the implications of this judgment to the woman? The tender-hearted woman, more than the man, sees her sorrow multiplied many times over during her child's infancy, growing up and even adulthood. Today, if sin were not present in both husband and wife, submission would not be an issue."

CONCLUSION

From today's lesson, what would you say is your present condition? Where would you like to be? Use the space below to record your answer. If you feel comfortable, you may discuss this with the group.

____

____

T Adam and Eve sinned by eating the forbidden fruit; now they would suffer in order to eat. Emphasize that the suffering, disease, and hunger we experience in the world today are as a result of a sin-cursed earth.

This lesson was not a pleasant picture of humanity, but God did not leave us hopeless. In the next lesson we will discover God's plan to restore us to purposeful, joyful living on earth, and the hope of future eternal happiness after we pass from this earth.

LESSON 3

ENTERING INTO MY NEW LIFE

INTRODUCTION

In last week's lesson we looked at the Scriptures to see God's intended design for mankind and discovered that we were created in a perfect state. We fell from that state of perfection when Adam disobeyed God. As a result, judgment fell on him and upon all creation. (Genesis 3:14-19) Adam and Eve were banished from the Garden of Eden and experienced both physical and spiritual death. Life on earth became toil, pain, and death. The good news is that God did not leave us there. He immediately promised that provision had been made for humankind to be restored to God's original design by sending His Son to pay for the penalty of our sin. This lesson will explore what the Bible says about receiving New Life to restore us to God's original design.

KEY VERSES

Isaiah 53:6 *We all, like sheep, have gone astray, each of us has turned to his own way; and the LORD has laid on him the iniquity of us all.*

1 Peter 2:24 *He himself (Jesus) bore our sins in his body on the tree, so that we might die to sins and live for righteousness; by his wounds you have been healed.*

I. QUALIFICATIONS FOR RECEIVING NEW LIFE

A. Repentance

1. We often hear people say, "I am pretty good. I have never broken any of the Ten Commandments. Why should I repent?" How would you answer such a person according to Isaiah 53:6, our Key Verse, as to why we need to repent?

____

____

S "We are not sinners because we sin—we sin because ***we are*** sinners."

2. Someone else may say, "What about those who have not heard that they are sinners? Are they responsible for their sin?" How does Romans 1:20 answer that?

____

S "Their condemnation is not their rejecting Christ of whom they have not heard; but on sinning against the light they have. For example, evolutionists and atheists must go against everything that God displays in nature. They seek to explain nature in terms of a 'big bang theory'. They refuse to listen to reason and reject clear evidence that surrounds them."

3. How important is repentance to receiving New Life? (Luke 13:2-3)

S "This passage teaches that death is a common denominator to everyone. Only repentance can bring life as people prepare to enter God's Kingdom of Light."

B. Giving Up Trusting in Ourselves

It is part of our nature to try to work our way to heaven or receiving New Life, but the Bible does not appear to leave any room for our own works.

1. How does God look at all our attempts to do good in order to receive eternal life? (Isaiah 64:6)

S "The best of humans are corrupt and polluted in comparison to our righteous God who cannot even look upon sin."

2. For what reason do our works not qualify us to be saved, that is, to receive New Life to make us fit us for heaven? (Ephesians 2:8,9)

S "The *basis* is grace, the *means* is faith. Faith is the only *means* by which we can accept God's *gift* of salvation. We are saved *by* His grace *through* our faith."

C. Trusting in Jesus as Our Sin-Bearer

1. According to our Key Verse (Isaiah 53:6) what responsibility has God taken to free us from our sins?

____

____

S "God has to punish sin to be a righteous God, so He laid the punishment of that iniquity (sin), not on the sheep who deserved it, but on Jesus, the Lamb of God, who died in their place."

2. The other Key Verse (1 Peter 2:24) describes how Jesus took our sins upon Himself. What did He have to do to pay for, and take our sins upon Himself?

____

____

S "By God judging our sins though Jesus' sacrifice, our sin-sick soul can be healed. Even our physical body experiences healing after we receive salvation. Is there someone here who has experienced a measure of healing from God?"

3. Although Jesus died for the sins of all mankind, not everyone will go to heaven. Repentance from our sins was the first condition. (See Matthew 3:2; 4:17; Luke 13:3,5) What is the next step needed without which there is no entry into heaven by anyone? (John 1:12)

____

S "To become His children, we must be born into His Kingdom. We do so by receiving Him into our lives as our personal Savior. This is the gift of New Birth. 'The spirit of man is the candle of the Lord.' (Proverbs 20:27) We must invite Jesus to light the candle of our spirit."

4. For many people, it is hard to accept that there is only one way to heaven, but the Bible makes no room for any other way. What is that way according to John 14:6?

____

S "Contrary to what many people think, salvation is not attained through many different ways. Jesus is the only way to the Father because He is the only One from the Father. (See John 1:1-2; 3:13) Jesus is the 'ladder' between heaven and earth with access to both realms."

5. Receiving Jesus into your life is the step that you must take to receive eternal life. Revelation 3:20 tells us how we can invite Him into our lives. Describe in your own words what you must do to receive Jesus.

____

____

S "This portion of Scripture teaches several principles:
1. Jesus will not force Himself upon us; we must invite Him in. The latch of the door is on the inside.
2. There will be no fellowship with God unless we have Him enter our heart and let Him become part of our lives."

II. TAKING THE STEP TO RECEIVE NEW LIFE

T To introduce this section, it may be important to explain once again what it means to become a Christian. Explain that we were born into Satan's kingdom under his rule. Receiving Christ gives us the privilege of citizenship in God's Kingdom of Light. Review the chart "The Two Spiritual Kingdoms Contrasted" which you reviewed in the Introductory Lesson. Do not force the issue of receiving Christ, but say that they may wish to consider the cost of becoming a disciple of Jesus Christ before they pray this prayer.

Many people have heard and understood the message of the Bible as to how to receive eternal life, but they have never entered in because they have not taken the step to repent of their sins and to receive the Lord Jesus into their hearts by faith. You are invited to consider the following prayer to see if it expresses what you sense God is inviting you to do to receive eternal life:

Lord Jesus, I admit that I am a sinner and do not deserve heaven or eternal life. My sins are undeniable and they condemn me. I now choose to repent of my sins and from trusting in my good works to merit salvation. I believe that Jesus' death on the cross paid for the penalty of my sins. Thank You for forgiving me. Come into my life and to mold me into the person You intended me to be. By faith, I believe that You have heard my prayer and received me as Your child. As a new citizen in Your Kingdom, help me to live the kind of

life You want me to live. Thank You, Father, for hearing my prayer. Amen.

If you sense God is leading you to pray this prayer, read it now as your personal prayer and seal that promise with your own hand by inserting the date and signing your name to remind yourself of your commitment. When Satan comes to tempt you and tells you that your commitment was not real, you simply have to turn to the place on this page and remind him of your total commitment to God, and he will flee from you. (James 4:7)

On (date) ______________________________________, I received Jesus Christ as my Savior and Lord, and I believe He has forgiven me of all my sins. I have promised to live for him as long as He gives me life. After I die, I will be with Him forever.

(My signature) ______________________________________

If you prayed this prayer, you are now a child of God and will have the privileges that belong to you as a new citizen in His Kingdom. In the next lesson we will explore how you can be sure you have eternal life, and the benefits that are yours as a child of God.

Now, write the name of a friend with whom you could share the commitment you have made.

Name: ______________________________ Phone: ____________________

You may wish to say something like this: "I have made a most wonderful decision! I have invited the Lord Jesus Christ into my life to become my personal Savior. I now have a personal relationship with Him, and when I die I will go to heaven!" This will strengthen your faith and give you a deeper assurance that you are a child of God.

T Explain what telling others about their inviting Jesus in their lives will do for them (Romans 10:9-10). When we confess Him as our Savior, that is heart faith. The result is salvation. These are not two separate steps to salvation; they belong together. Also, explain the importance of telling someone the significant decision you have made in inviting Jesus into your life.

LESSON 4

KNOWING AND CLAIMING MY INHERITANCE AS A CHILD OF GOD

S "Before we start with Lesson 4, let's review the previous lessons:

Introductory Lesson: We learned the spiritual world has two kingdoms: the Kingdom of Darkness and the Kingdom of Light. We were all born into the Kingdom of Darkness."

Lesson 1: We were trying to assess our needs and where we were spiritually."

Lesson 2: We learned that man was created perfect, but through Adam we fell and are all born into the Kingdom of Darkness."

Lesson 3: We discovered that in order to pass from the Kingdom of Darkness to the Kingdom of Light, we had to repent of our sins and receive Jesus Christ as our personal Savior. We had to yield control of our own life to Jesus."

INTRODUCTION

Every kingdom on earth has its privileges and responsibilities that are embedded in their constitutions and their laws. When you received Jesus Christ as your Savior and Lord you became a citizen of the Kingdom of Heaven and received the privilege to be part of all the benefits and responsibilities that belong to that Kingdom. This is a most exciting and life-long process which the Bible calls "growing in Christ".

In this lesson you will discover what the Bible says about how you can confidently trust in the fact that you now have eternal life, and how you can receive the great benefits available to you as a citizen in the Kingdom of Heaven. These benefits begin now and last throughout eternity. Let us explore this great adventure you have just begun.

KEY VERSES

1 John 5:11-13 *[11]And this is the testimony: God has given us eternal life, and this life is in His Son. [12]He who has the Son has life; he who does not have the Son of God does not have life. [13]I write these things to you who believe in the name of the Son of God so that you may know that you have eternal life.*

2 Corinthians 5:17 *Therefore, if anyone is in Christ, he is a new creation; the old has gone, the new has come!*

I. THE BASIS AND BENEFIT OF FORGIVEN SINS

A. The Basis on Which I Can Claim Forgiveness for My Sins

1. What part does Jesus have in the forgiveness of sins? (Acts 13:38-39)

____

____

S "There is absolutely nothing we can do for the forgiveness of our sins. Let's look at Acts 2:38."

2. It is sometimes difficult to imagine how gracious God is in forgiving our sins. What does God do with even our worst sins? (Isaiah 1:18)

____

____

S "Trusting in religious rituals will not do. See Isaiah 1:10-15. We must meet three conditions: admit our sin, ask forgiveness, make an about-turn (repent), and accept His forgiveness."

3. What is it that purifies us from all sin? (1 John 1:7)

____

____

S "John did not say here, 'Walk ***according*** to the light' but 'walk ***in*** the light.' Walking according to the light would require sinless perfection and would make fellowship with God impossible for sinful humans. However, 'to walk ***in*** the light' suggests, instead, openness and responsiveness to the light as we appropriate the blood of Jesus cleansing us from every sin. The bottom line is having right attitudes of love, which are acceptable to God, not the accomplishment of perfect conduct. According to Ephesians 4:13-14, the goal is towards an unblemished character which has moral and spiritual integrity in relationship to God."

B. Benefits of Forgiven Sins

1. What does Acts 26:17-18 say is the benefit of receiving forgiveness of sins?

____

____

____

S "Where do you now have power to do or not to do that which you had no control over before you became a Christian?"

2. What characteristics of Jesus give you all the benefits of your new life as a Christian? (Acts 15:11)

____

____

S "Grace is God giving us what we do not deserve, not our trying to work to earn His favor in order to enjoy the benefits He offers."

3. In what way do you sense Jesus has granted you grace (has been gracious to you)?

____

____

T It may be fitting here to give your testimony as to where you sense God has been gracious to you. Your transparency will encourage others to share.

4. Not only do you benefit from what God gives you when you have new life, but the greatest benefit comes from your new identity. According to 2 Corinthians 5:17, who are you now as a Christian?

____

____

Following are two columns. The one on the left describes who you once were before you became a Christian. After reading Ephesians 2:11-22, fill in the right column with descriptions of who you are now in Christ. You will discover that these are opposites.

	Who I was without God		**Who I am now in Christ**
v. 12	Separate from Christ, foreigners and without hope	v. 13	
v. 14	Wall of hostility and anger between us and God	vs.15 & 16	
v. 19	Foreigners and aliens	v. 19	
v. 19	Part of Satan's household	vs. 21 & 22	

Note: These are only a few of the benefits that we enjoy in our new life as a Christian. As you read God's Word and continue on in these classes you will discover many deep treasures that you may claim as yours.

CONCLUSION

Many new Christians have a very basic question to ask in regards to feelings. For example, they will say, "What if I do not feel like a Christian? Am I still a Christian?" Let us look at some key verses in the Scriptures to consider this subject.

1. What determines whether or not you are a Christian? See Key Verse 1 John 5:11-12.

____

____

S "There are only two kinds of people in the world: those who have Jesus, and those who do not have Jesus. This is a concept of which we must not lose sight. Many think people of other faiths, who are sincere, will also make it to heaven. According to God's Word, this is false."

2. Instead of feelings, what other indicator does God give you that Jesus is in your life according to Romans 8:16 and 1 John 3:24? In what way have you experienced the sense that the Spirit of God is living in you?

____

____

T Expect answers like: "I have a sense of peace, hope, freedom from guilt, etc." All these are also indications of being born again.

3. According to Romans 10:9-10, what must you do to receive a greater assurance that you are a child of God?

____

____

4. In obedience to the statement in Romans 10:9-10, with whom will you share the fact that you now are a Christian? This is a very important step to sensing that you have entered the New Life as a Christian.

T Suggest someone whom they know is a Christian and who would be happy for them.

As you progress in the study of the Word of God and share with others what God has done in your life, you will receive a greater confidence and assurance that you are a child of God.

In the next lesson, we will discover our new responsibilities and privileges in the Kingdom of God, as we share with others the truth of our inheritance in Jesus Christ.

LESSON 5

RESPONSIBILITIES AND PRIVILEGES IN MY NEW KINGDOM

INTRODUCTION

The Old Testament tells of an event where the city of Samaria was besieged by an army until the whole city was starving. Outside the city gates were some lepers who were not permitted to go into the city because of their disease. They, too, were starving. Their only hope of finding food was to go to the besieging army's camp to see if they would be merciful to them and give them food. They had nothing to lose, so they went. When they came to the camp, it was totally deserted except for the horses and donkeys and all the supplies. The lepers were delighted and ate all they could, plus stored away extra supplies. They realized there was food for the whole starving city and began to feel guilty that they had more than enough and inside the city the people were starving. So they decided to tell them of the abundant food supply. The whole city was fed and saved from starvation. (You will find this account in 2 Kings 7)

Leprosy in the Bible is a symbol of sin. We, in our sinful state, were without God and without hope in this world. Then Jesus searched us out and saved us and placed us into His Kingdom where there is more than enough for all of us—freedom, forgiveness, a new beginning, spiritual food, and much more. Just like these lepers, we have the privilege and responsibility to share how we found New Life. When we tell others how we found the Lord Jesus as our Savior, we are simply one beggar telling another beggar where we found bread. Telling others of how you came to this New Life as a Christian is known as **witnessing.**

S "Witnessing is telling others what you have experienced."

In this lesson, we will discover what the Bible has to say about our responsibility as a Christian to tell others what God has done for us. Also, we will learn about some tools and how to use them to share our faith.

KEY VERSES

Acts 1:8 "*But you will receive power when the Holy Spirit comes on you; and you will be my witnesses in Jerusalem, and in all Judea and Samaria, and to the ends of the earth.*"

Matthew 28:18-20 *18Then Jesus came to them and said, "All authority in heaven and on earth has been given to me. 19Therefore go and make disciples of all nations, baptizing them in the name of the Father and of the Son and of the*

Holy Spirit, [20]and teaching them to obey everything I have commanded you. And surely I am with you always, to the very end of the age."

I. WHAT DOES THE BIBLE SAY ABOUT OUR RESPONSIBILITY TO SHARE?

In Acts 1:8, before Jesus left this earth to go back to heaven, he told the disciples that the Holy Spirit would come upon them after He left. The fulfillment of that event is recorded in Acts 2. The Spirit of Jesus, the Holy Spirit entered your life when you became a Christian. That is, He is now resident in your life.

A. According to Acts 1:8, by whose power will you be witnessing?

____

S "Satan does not like us to share the Good News with others. What does he use in our lives to try to neutralize the impact or keep us from witnessing?"

B. According to Acts 1:8, how did Jesus envision getting the gospel to the ends of the earth?

____

____

____

C. Matthew 28:18-20 is known as The Great Commission. What does this command of Jesus tell us to do?

____

____

S "It is very clear in Scripture that new disciples must be taught, that is, they must submit themselves to the teaching of God's Word."

From the above verses, two things stand out clearly when it comes to witnessing:

1. It is the responsibility of everyone to witness.
2. We must not do that in our own power. God will do the witnessing through us by the power of His Holy Spirit working in us.

The next section will give you two important tools to enable you to witness to those who do not yet know Jesus as their Lord and Savior.

II. TWO EFFECTIVE TOOLS FOR PERSONAL EVANGELISM

A. The Witnessing Booklet, *From Darkness to Light* (available at foundations4living.ca/bookstore) If this booklet is not available, you may use *The Four Spiritual Laws* or similar material.

B. The Proper Use of the Personal Testimony

1. Why give your personal testimony?

    a. It is the first tool needed to be an effective witness — three times in the book of Acts Paul gives his testimony.

T You may wish to refer to Acts 22:1-21.

    b. It gives you assurance that you are born again. (Romans 10:9-10)

    c. It gives you credibility.

    d. Your vulnerability invites their vulnerability.

2. The testimony includes three essential elements:

    a. what I was before I became a citizen of God's Kingdom.

    b. what my new citizenship has meant to me (how it has changed me and given me purpose and fulfilment).

    c. how one can transfer from the Kingdom of Darkness to the Kingdom of Light.

3. How not to give a testimony:

    a. using words that the non-Christian does not understand.

    b. describing your past life in detail.

    c. not saying enough on how your life is different.

4. Pointers on writing your personal testimony:

    a. In talking about your past life, seek to identify with the person to whom you are witnessing.

    b. Emphasize clearly how your life has changed—regarding your habits, fears, emotions, lifestyle, and in regards to the Word of God

    c. Mention the positive aspects of becoming a Christian.

5. Use the Testimony Worksheet page and write your testimony using the given outline.

TESTIMONY WORKSHEET

For those who received Jesus as an adult

"There was a time in my life..." (Complete this sentence and tell what your life was like before you came to know Jesus as your personal Savior. Use only a few concepts. Be sure you illustrate at least one concept with a specific example from your life.)

"Now that I know I am a citizen of God's Kingdom..." (Now state how your life has changed using the reverse of what you said above. Also give specific examples of how your life is different. End your testimony with your assurance of salvation: "I'm so glad that I now know that I would go to heaven when I die.)

At the end of your testimony say, ***"May I share with you how I discovered what it means to be a Christian and to have eternal life? This little booklet says it in a nutshell. Let's go through it together."***

Then read the booklet, *From Darkness to Light.* Follow the guidelines titled, "How to Present *From Darkness to Light* booklet". (page 32)

TESTIMONY WORKSHEET

For one converted early in childhood

1. Begin with, ***"I'm so glad that I am a citizen of God's Kingdom."***

2. State one benefit.

3. Illustrate your benefit with a specific example from your experience.

4. Always include, ***"I am so grateful that I now know that I am a Christian and have eternal life."***

5. Transitional statement: ***"Would you mind if I shared with you the answer to the most important question in life? How can I know for certain that I am a Christian? This little booklet says it in a nutshell. Could we go through it together?"***

6. Then read together the booklet ***From Darkness to Light*** and follow the guidelines as suggested on the next page titled, *How to Present "From Darkness to Light"*. (on the next page)

HOW TO PRESENT
"FROM DARKNESS TO LIGHT"

which illustrates how you can transfer from the Kingdom of Darkness to the Kingdom of Light

1. Purpose not to argue. Be sure you will leave with a favorable attitude, so the person you are sharing with will welcome the opportunity to talk with you again.
2. Do not be pushy. Be sensitive as to whether the Holy Spirit has prepared this person to receive the gospel.
3. If people say they are not interested, respect their decision.
4. If questions come up during reading *From Darkness to Light* booklet, say, "That's a good question. Let's talk about it after we have finished going through this booklet".
5. Hold the booklet and point to the line you are reading so your partner can follow easily, or you may each have a booklet.
6. If there seems to be no response, stop and ask, "Does this make sense to you?" Then go over it again.
7. Use the person's name as you go through the booklet.
8. If you share the booklets with a group, the whole group may wish to pray the prayer. If there is only one response you may wish to do it privately.
9. Be a good listener. This will help you give right answers.
10. Always be courteous and respect their answers and decisions.
11. Make sure you ask the questions in the booklet, and then wait for their answers. At this point, don't try to correct them.

CONCLUSION

In the coming weeks, we will seek to share our faith using these tools and discussing the results from obeying God's command to fulfilling the Great Commission.

If you want to share your testimony to a wider audience, you can email it to Foundations for Living Society at info@foundations4living.ca

LESSON 6

GROWING IN MY NEW LIFE AND ENJOYING IT

T If you are dealing with new Christians, remember: they are like soft clay in your hands. You will need to help build them a solid foundation upon which they can grow in their new Christian life.

INTRODUCTION

You have just begun a relationship with the dearest Friend you could ever meet in the Person of Jesus Christ. He has given you a new beginning by forgiving your sin, and entering your life in the Person of the Holy Spirit. The Holy Spirit is the Spirit of Jesus now residing in you. It is He that gives you the power to change, making you more into the kind of person God wants you to be and you desire to be. You now have a new Master and are under a new Kingdom with all its privileges and responsibilities. You will want to know how you can continue to grow in intimacy with God, your new King, and enjoy the privileges and responsibilities of the new Kingdom.

KEY VERSES

Matthew 7:24-25 [24] *"Therefore everyone who hears these words of mine and puts them into practice is like a wise man who built his house on the rock.* [25]*The rain came down, the streams rose, and the winds blew and beat against that house; yet it did not fall, because it had its foundation on the rock."*

1 Corinthians 3:10b,11 [10]*...but each one should be careful how he builds.* [11]*For no one can lay any foundation other than the one already laid, which is Jesus Christ.*

I. OBEDIENCE: THE FIRST STEP TO BUILDING YOUR NEW LIFE IN GOD'S KINGDOM

A. Following a New Master

Before you received Jesus Christ as your Savior, you were going your own way and doing your own thing following the ways of Satan. You discovered this to be self-destructive without lasting fulfilment, but now as a follower of Christ you have the opportunity to build a new life.

1. According to the Key Verse, Matthew 7:24, when does God's Word help you to build your New Life solidly?

____

S "One of the great perils for us Christians is that we obey less than what we know. This results in hardening of our hearts to the Word of God. Often you hear people say, "This is not deep enough for me." They may simply want more head knowledge to tickle their ears. What they likely need is to obey what they know in order that they can grow."

2. Paraphrase what Matthew 7:25 says is the benefit of building up your life as described in Matthew 7:24.

S "When my faith sustains me in the storm, it will be a great testimony to believers and unbelievers alike."

3. You may wish to share what storms or difficulties you were not able to bear before.

T Your students might find it helpful if you would share storms you found hard to weather before you became a Christian.

B. Knowing the Foundation Upon Which to Build

1. Your Foundation Stone is Jesus Christ, as you see in our second Key Verse. What would be a practical example of building your life on the foundation of Jesus? You may get some help from 1 Timothy 6:17-19.

S "Those of us who have had a lot of destructive habits or a sinful past will have to remove 'debris' or remnants by receiving forgiveness through confession and repentance before we can build upon a solid foundation."

2. There are a number of ways you can discover what the Word of God says that will enable you to follow it. Read the following verses and write the word that tells you how you can know the Word of God:

   a) Romans 10:17 ____________________

S "This kind of hearing is understanding that produces action."

   b) Revelation 1:3 ____________________

S "Reading is important because it can bring about change in our lives."

   c) Psalm 119:11 ____________________

S "Knowing the Word protects us from wrong actions in times of crisis."

   d) Psalm 1:2-3 ____________________

S "If applied, the Word brings peace and tranquility into our lives in times of good and difficult times."

II. WHAT DOES OBEDIENCE TO THE WORD DO FOR ME?

From the story of the conversion of Paul in the New Testament to the present, there are millions of testimonies of people from every tribe and nation who have received the Lord Jesus Christ as their Savior and become obedient to the word of God. They have exchanged their destructive habits of addictions, immorality, and hatred, for lives filled with joy, purpose, love and purity.

A. What do the following Scriptures say the Word of God will do to transform us?

1. 1 Peter 2:2-3 ____________________

S "True rebirth is demonstrated by a thirst for God's Word and a desire to obey it. That is why immediate discipleship after conversion is imperative."

2. Hebrews 4:12 ____________________

S "In other words, God's Word enables us to judge our own motives and desires to recognize what is of the flesh or of the Spirit."

3. 2 Timothy 3:16-17 ____________________

S "All of us need the Word of God constantly in our daily living to correct, rebuke, and guide us so we can discern the devil's trying to lure us off the track."

4. Romans 12:2 ______________________________

S "Before we can be transformed, we must reject the mould into which the world tries to put us. What do you sense is that worldly mould that you feel squeezed into?"

5. Joshua 1:8______________________________

S "What do you think would be success in God's eyes?"

Note: As you continue to study the Word of God you will discover many more benefits.

B. Share with the group how the Word of God is beginning to transform your life; or share a specific example of obedience to the Word which brought you great blessing.

T Share how the Word of God has transformed your life as you sense this would help the others to share. Always connect obedience with the Word—Why do we connect with the boss? To get instructions!

III. THE SEARCH FOR INNER PEACE IS ENDED THROUGH OBEDIENCE

A. For what two reasons does Isaiah say that he rejoices in God in Isaiah 61:10?

____

____

____

____

S "My purpose and joy comes from knowing who God is and who I am in Christ."

B. Whose joy do we experience through obedience? (John 15:10-11)

____

____

S "Our love for God and others depends on our obedience to God and His Word. As a result, our joy will radiate from us."

CONCLUSION

Record or share any steps you must take in response to today's lesson.

S "What joy are you experiencing in your Christian Life?"

LESSON 7

THE HOLY SPIRIT: THE NEW LIFE WITHIN ME

T This lesson deals with another key biblical concept that is most often attacked by false belief systems and their promoters, that is, that **the Holy Spirit is a person**, not an "it" or a "force".

INTRODUCTION

In our last lesson, we learned that when we receive the Lord Jesus into our lives, He comes to indwell us through the Holy Spirit. In this lesson, we will seek to explore *who* the Holy Spirit is and what role *He* plays in the life of the believer. The Scriptures clearly declare that the Holy Spirit is as the third Person of the Trinity (God in three Persons). He is also the expression of God in you. This concept is beyond the scope of this lesson, but it will be covered in another class.

S "Notice that the Holy Spirit is not an 'it' but is addressed by pronouns like, 'he' and 'who'. Let's look at Ephesians 4:30."

The Holy Spirit is not just an "energy" or "vital force" which many cults and occult religions describe by names such as "spirit guides" or the "Great Spirit" and others. We will discover that He is the very life of God in you, which enables you to live the kind of life God wants you to live and you desire to live.

KEY VERSES

John 14:26 *"But the Counsellor, the Holy Spirit, whom the Father will send in my name, will teach you all things and will remind you of everything I have said to you."*

S "The Holy Spirit is a powerful person on our side, working for and with us. 'Counsellor' combines the idea of comfort and counsel."

Ezekiel 36:27 *"And I will put my Spirit in you and move you to follow my decrees and be careful to keep my laws."*

S "No matter how impure your life is, God offers you a fresh start by giving you a new heart. This is what becoming 'a new creation' means. (2 Corinthians 5:17)"

S "**Nugget:** There is always a new beginning with God."

S "Question: Why patch up your old life when you can have a new one?"

I. THE HOLY SPIRIT IN RELATION TO THE BELIEVER

A. Study Romans 8:9

1. Where is the Holy Spirit in relation to the believer (Christian)?

2. What if the Holy Spirit does not live within us?

B. After reading John 14:16-17, explain:

1. Why the world or non-believer does not have the Holy Spirit

S "Spiritual things are understood only by those who have the Holy Spirit living in them. This is one of the reasons the ungodly world does not understand our thinking, lifestyle, or decisions we make."

2. The unbeliever's inability to follow or understand God's laws

S "Here is why we cannot dictate how unbelievers should live. The unbeliever does not have the power to do or even understand the godly principles of life."

II. THE ROLE OF THE HOLY SPIRIT IN YOUR LIFE

A. According to your Key Verse, Ezekiel 36:27

1. What function does the Holy Spirit have in the believer?

S "If someone who professes to be a Christian does not want to or does not have the power to live the Christian life, one has to question whether that person is a Christ-follower."

2. What changes have you personally noticed in the power you now

have to live the kind of life God wants you to live?

T Here you may wish to give an example from your life where you were once powerless and how Jesus helps you now in this area of your life.

B. Romans 8:16 gives a very important function of the Holy Spirit in the new believer.

1. What is that?

S "It is important to recognize that only you know for sure you are a Christian. It is also true that others also recognize the Holy Spirit in others."

2. What evidence do you sense you have that you are a Christian?

T Listen for comments like: "I have peace I never had before" or "I sense that I have been freed from the power of guilt", etc.

C. How will the believer know the truth among so much false teaching in the world? Consider John 16:13.

1. What is another name for the Holy Spirit?

T You may wish to point out another name, the Counsellor. (John 14:16)

2. What part will the Holy Spirit have in guiding you through life?

S "It usually takes time and experience to recognize the voice of the Holy Spirit."

3. Consider John 16:14. We are often exposed to false teachings by other belief systems. These often give glory to the man who either

founded the cult or one who subscribes to its teaching. What role does the Holy Spirit have in helping you discern what is right?

D. What other role does the Holy Spirit have according to the following Scriptures?

1. Acts 1:8

S "To witness, we will need to engage the will to obey when God, through the Holy Spirit, prompts us to witness for Him."

2. John 14:26 (Key Verse)

S "When have you experienced this since you have become a Christian?"

3. John 16:8

4. How does the role of conviction of our sin by the Holy Spirit help the believer to retain his intimate relationship with God? (1 John 1:6-7)

S "A person walking in sin cannot have true fellowship with others. True fellowship requires walking in the light (being transparent and open with our lives)."

III. APPLICATION

A. What ministry of the Holy Spirit dealt with in this lesson has been most meaningful to you?

____

____

T You could expect some of these concepts: "The fact that I can daily depend on the Holy Spirit's work in me, to guide me into all truth; to depend on Him to speak through me (not my own words) and do only those things that would please Him; to give me discernment to understand what I should do. My desire is to bring glory to Jesus."

B. What do you sense is an issue that the Holy Spirit has been prompting you to deal with? You may wish to discuss this with your class or some other person with whom you could feel safe.

____

____

____

____

T Listen for comments like desiring to receive power and freedom to witness wherever they are prompted to do so. Also, a desire to live in a manner pleasing to God.

CONCLUSION

Today's lesson dealt with the Holy Spirit being resident in you. There is another very important aspect of the Holy Spirit's work in you. He not only wants to be **Resident**, but He wants to be **President**. We will deal with this very exciting aspect next week.

LESSON 8

THE HOLY SPIRIT: RESIDENT OR PRESIDENT?

INTRODUCTION

In our last lesson we learned about the Holy Spirit taking up residence in our hearts when we accepted Jesus Christ as our Savior. He has become our companion and friend for life. The process we go through when Jesus first enters our life can be more clearly illustrated by a simple example:

> **S** "Word-pictures are powerful tools in teaching spiritual truths. Let us look at this life situation to teach an important spiritual truth."

Picture yourself driving a car along the highway of life with you in the driver's seat. You come across a hitch-hiker who seems really nice and pleasant-looking. You cannot resist picking him up and so, you do. As you travel along, you discover that the hitch-hiker is none other than Jesus Christ. You have just barely begun driving when He says to you, "The vehicle you are driving actually belongs to me. If you stay at the wheel you will soon crash. Will you pull over and let Me drive? I promise to take you safely to wherever you want to go. That is an absolute guarantee."

You know your own driving record has been disastrous, so you stop and let Him take the wheel. You soon discover the great freedom and peace of mind you now have. This Driver knows where you want to go and how to get there. He also gets you there safely. Now you don't want anyone else to take you.

Up to this point you may not have realized that Jesus does not only want to be Resident (Passenger) but President (Driver) of your life. God knows that sinful human nature always crashes when we think we can do it on our own. Self-destruction is the end result. Today's lesson will explore what the Scriptures have to say about Jesus in the Person of the Holy Spirit, becoming more than Savior in your life. He also wants to be President, Driver, and Lord of our lives. If Jesus is your Co-pilot, it's time to exchange seats!

> **S** "Our own rationalization does not meet God's standard of the Holy Spirit's guidance."

KEY VERSES

1 Corinthians 6:19-20 *19Do you not know that your body is a temple of the Holy Spirit, who is in you whom you have received from God? 20You are not your own; you were bought with a price. Therefore honor God with your body.*

1 Corinthians 3:16-17 [16]*Don't you know that you yourselves are God's temple and that God's Spirit lives in you?* [17]*If anyone destroys God's temple, God will destroy him; for God's temple is sacred, and you are that temple.*

I. BASIS UPON WHICH GOD CAN CLAIM OWNERSHIP OF OUR LIVES

In many world religions, human life appears to be cheap. Children by the thousands have been sacrificed to destroy land mines. Many are being used for cheap labor, and men and women have been slaughtered to effect ethnic cleansing. This is not God's view of mankind. God puts the highest value on humanity and desires to make us whole. (See Mark 8:36-37) You are precious to Him. He has made a provision for you to receive the Holy Spirit to become your gracious Lord and lifelong Companion.

A. God's View of Our Bodies

1. Upon what basis does God claim to have ownership of our bodies? (1 Corinthians 6:19-20)

____

____

> **S** "Here is one reason why taking a human life is so morally wrong. In the light of this, how would God see abortion and euthanasia? Society says, 'We have a right to our own bodies.' They think this is freedom, but actually they are enslaved to their own passions and desires."

2. What is there in man that makes him so highly treasured by God? (1 Corinthians 3:16)

____

____

____

3. How severe is God's judgment upon those who seek to destroy this "temple of the living God" which is your body? (1 Corinthians 3:16)

____

____

> **S** "Let's look at Proverbs 28:17. How is a murderer destroyed?"

B. God's Reason for Owning and Possessing Our Bodies

1. God promised the Holy Spirit in the Old Testament as found in Ezekiel 36:26-27. For what reason did He want man to be filled with the Holy Spirit?

____

____

____

2. Since having received the Lord Jesus Christ as your Savior, what areas of your life have you found most difficult to deal with?

____

____

____

____

T Seek to make this a time of sharing if the group is open to it. You may wish to begin with your own testimony.

3. God knows that we can not handle life very well on our own. Paul, who was a Christian at the time of this writing, describes his struggles with life in Romans 7:14-25. Consider this set of verses and complete the sentence or phrase taken from this passage:

   a. The law is spiritual, I am ____________.
   b. I do not ____________ what I do.
   c. What I want to do I ___ ______ ___, but what I hate I ___ .
   d. It is no longer I that do it but ____ ________ _____ in me.
   e. I know that ______ ________ ________ in me, that is, my sinful nature.

S "Becoming a Christian does not take away our desire and inclination to sin nor does it exempt us from temptation."

4. From Paul's observation he saw two laws at work in his life. What were they? (Romans 7:21-23)

S "Salvation (being born again) takes but a moment of faith and surrender. Becoming more and more like Jesus is a lifelong process."

a.

S "This means that we are more loyal to our old ways of selfish living than to God."

b.

S "This law instructs us to be loyal to the New Life within us."

5. Paul recognized that it was not God's design for him that he should live in this state of defeat. What did he see as the answer? (v. 25)

S "Thank God that He has given you freedom and victory through Jesus Christ."

6. From where did Paul see that he would be able to get the power to have control over his sinful nature? (Romans 8:9)

Note: From the study above, we have observed that God's reason for owning and possessing our body, mind, and soul is that we might be made whole and serve Him. Unless God has total control of our bodies and minds through the Holy Spirit who indwells us, we will continue to live defeated lives. How can we then give the Holy Spirit the "driver's seat" or the presidency of our lives?

S "There is a tendency to treat the filling of the Holy Spirit as magic or a quick-fix procedure to give us the ability to speak in tongues, healing powers, or spiritual superiority. This is not what the Bible teaches, but rather, there are conditions or prerequisites that we must meet to be filled with the Holy Spirit."

II. HOW CAN WE MAKE GOD THE HOLY SPIRIT PRESIDENT OF OUR LIVES?

A. What are God's conditions for us to be filled with the Holy Spirit?

1. To whom will God give the Holy Spirit? Acts 5:32

2. The sinful nature with its old habits wants to continue to cling to us as we try to live the Christian life. Before we can be filled with the Holy Spirit, what must we do about this sin clinging to us? (Colossians 3:5-9)

Note: "Putting to death" or "putting off" is done by confessing this sin and receiving forgiveness. You will see from the following verses in Colossians 3 that God does not want you to remain spiritually "dead" or "naked". When our will has been surrendered and our sin dealt with, we are candidates to be "clothed" or filled with the Holy Spirit.

B. How can I be filled with the Holy Spirit?

1. Once I have met the conditions of surrendering my will and "putting to death the deeds of the flesh" I can do what Luke 11:11-13 invites me to do. What is that?

2. The other terms for "receiving" the Holy Spirit are "put on", or "clothe yourself with" as used in Colossians 3:12-13. According to these verses, what virtues will then characterize us when the Holy Spirit becomes President of our lives?

3. Once you have asked the Holy Spirit to take over and fill you as you were invited to do in Luke 11:11-13, thank God daily for the Holy Spirit's life in you and daily ask Him to fill you anew. What will the Holy Spirit then enable you to do?

a. Acts 1:8

____

b. Galatians 5:22-23

____

____

CONCLUSION

If you have recognized that without the Holy Spirit being President of your life, you cannot live the Christian life on your own, you are invited to pray this prayer in faith, and God will do what He has promised in Luke 11:11-13. When you invite Him in, He will come in and fill you to enable you to live a life of victory and fruitful service. The following is a suggested prayer:

> **"Lord Jesus, I thank You for receiving me as Your child and living in me through the Holy Spirit. I recognize that I have been sitting at the "driver's seat" and that sin has been clinging to me. I have not been able to live the victorious Christian life on my own. I now surrender my will and my life to You, and ask You to fill me with your Holy Spirit. I want Him to empower me daily to live for You and to serve You in whatever way You see fit. I thank You for answering my prayer. In Jesus name I thank You."**

Note: You may not feel any different after this prayer. Remember, that you do not live your life on feelings but on the basis of the Word of God. Ask God to empower you to do the daily tasks and to resist the temptations that you will face. You will discover the changes that God will make in your life. Next week we will deal with the subject of **How to Enjoy My Daily Walk in the Spirit.** Once you have been empowered by the Holy Spirit, you will want to know how to walk or live as a Spirit-filled Christian.

T Summarize Part II, How Can We Make God the Holy Spirit President of Our Lives? for your students.

S "Be willing to deal with the following initially and on an ongoing basis:

- **Surrender** (Romans 12:1-2) I reject the mold—mindsets and ways of living—which the world wants to put me in.
- **Sin** (1 John 1:9; Acts 5:32) I admit my needs and struggles, confess my sins, and walk in obedience.
- **Self** (Galatians 2:20; 2 Corinthians 5:14-15) I crucify my self-centeredness.
- **Spirit's filling** (Luke 11:11-13) I clothe myself with the Holy Spirit."

LESSON 9

WALKING IN THE SPIRIT THROUGH THE GREAT EXCHANGE PROGRAM

INTRODUCTION

Life is often pictured as a road on which we walk. Our road began in the Kingdom of Darkness under the tyranny of Satan. He held us in bondage where we had no power over our sinful habits that led to self-destruction and eternal damnation. When we received Jesus along this road, we crossed over from the Kingdom of Darkness into the Kingdom of Light. On this New Kingdom road, we discovered our Companion in the Person of the Holy Spirit, the Spirit of Jesus. He offers to exchange the things that still bind or enslave us for new garments that will bring us freedom and victory. This lesson will show us how we can continue to "walk in the Spirit" where we may shed the habits of the Kingdom of Darkness in exchange for freedom and purpose along this road of life.

S "Imagine for a moment that you (with all your imperfections) are walking on a road which runs through perfect surroundings. Along this road are "exchange shops" where you can trade your imperfections for perfection, say for example, your impatience for patience. At what exchange shops would you stop?

This is precisely what the Holy Spirit offers the Christian. Now, think about your answers: was your exchange external or internal? This lesson has good news for each one of us."

KEY VERSES

1 Peter 2:9 *But you are a chosen people, a royal priesthood, a holy nation, a people belonging to God, that you may declare the praises of Him who called you out of darkness into His wonderful light.*

John 8:31-32 *31 "If you hold to my teaching, you are really my disciples. 32 Then you will know the truth, and the truth will set you free."*

S "As we just read in 1 Peter 2:9, God sees you as a person He has chosen. You didn't choose Him; He chose you. See John 15:16."

I. THE GREAT EXCHANGE PROGRAM

A. Keeping Short Accounts with God

As a new Christian, you have already discovered that you are daily confronted with sin. What you desire, what you see, what you read, or actions or reactions you had may smudge your clean walk with God. If the sins you commit during the day remain with you, your fellowship with God and other people is broken and we miss out on experiencing the fullness and freedom of God. He has made provision for our daily cleansing. 1 John 1:5-9 gives us the solution to a daily walk with God and other people in our lives.

S "It is important that we do not approach this lesson on the basis of guilt, but on the basis of opportunity for exchange."

1. The first step to a daily cleansing is to admit that we are in need of cleansing. What are the consequences of not admitting our sin? (1 John 1:5-9)

   a. v. 6

   ____

   ____

   b. v. 8

   ____

   ____

   c. v. 10

   ____

   ____

S "Why must we confess our sins? (v. 9) When we confess, we agree with God regarding our sin, and that we are willing to turn from sin (repent). This way, we don't hide our sins from God (and from ourselves). We recognize our tendency to sin and our need to rely on His power to overcome sin."

2. The word "confess" in verse 9 also means "agree with". What are the results when we agree with God about our sin?

   ____

   ____

3. What is the benefit of our daily confession or agreeing with God about our sin? (v. 7)

   ____

S "Sin short-circuits fellowship with God and other Christians."

This cleansing from sin as soon as you are aware of the sin is known as "keeping short accounts with God." That makes you a daily candidate for **the Great Exchange Program** that Jesus offers everyone who comes to Him for salvation.

B. Jesus Is The Author Of The Great Exchange Program

Luke 4:18-21 tells us that Isaiah 61:1-3 is a description of what Jesus came to do for us. You will discover the great truths which bring freedom and purpose to every life that chooses to enter the Great Exchange Program with Jesus. Consider this passage in Isaiah and answer the following questions:

1. From verse 1, what good news is Jesus to deliver?

   a. ____________________

   b. ____________________

   c. ____________________

2. Making the Good News of Jesus Practical

   a. What will He do for the broken-hearted? (Psalm 34:18 and 51:17)

   ____

S "When trouble strikes, don't get frustrated with God. Instead, admit you need God's help and thank Him for being by your side."

   b. What kind of freedom from captivity could Jesus be talking about? (Romans 6:17-18 and 8:1-2)

   ____

   ____

   c. What will set us free? (John 8:32)

   ____

   ____

T You may wish to use another version of the Bible like the King James or Amplified versions to get a few more concepts of the Great Exchange principle.

Giving us freedom from bondage, light for darkness is only the first part of the Great Exchange Program. Let us consider other aspects that can bring wholeness and meaning to our lives.

3. In Isaiah 61:3 we see three exchanges available to us. What are they?

   a. For ashes He will give us ______________________

   b. For mourning He will give us ______________________

   c. For a spirit of despair He will give us ______________________

II. MAKING THE GREAT EXCHANGE PROGRAM PRACTICAL

The practical walk in the Spirit is continuously exchanging our weaknesses, our burdens, our sins, or our bondage, etc., for whatever we have need. With one hand we **release** our sin, burden, or bondage, and with the other hand we **receive** from God that which we have need of in exchange for that which we have released or confessed to Him. This is a delightful way to live — **Release and Receive.**

Suppose you have a great fear of getting a disease which you cannot shake. Here is what you can do: you can pray a prayer that would go something like this: **"Lord, you know my fear of getting (name the disease). I now release this fear to you and receive peace and health in exchange."**

List the areas of bondage, fear, sin, or whatever weakness that seems to defeat you. Then begin praying a prayer similar to the one above. God will give you great freedom and bring you to wholeness.

Here is my list:

Here is my prayer: Lord, you know my ______________________ .

I now release ______________________ and receive ______________________ in exchange. I thank you for hearing my prayer. Fill me afresh with your Holy Spirit to empower me to continue to live in victory.

CONCLUSION

Where appropriate, be prepared to share with your class where God has given you victory.

LESSON 10

SPIRITUAL HEALTH AND THE WORD OF GOD

INTRODUCTION

The Bible is often described as a "good book", a book with beautiful sayings, with examples of excellent literature. That is true of the Bible, but there is much more. By now you have discovered it is a book of unchangeable truths and is 100 percent reliable. The Word is life-producing and life-changing. Our very spiritual health depends on how we center our lives in the Word. George Mueller, a great man of faith, used to say, "Our vigor (or health) of our spiritual life will be in exact proportion to the place the Bible has in our life and thoughts." Dwight L. Moody, the great evangelist, used to say that the Scriptures were not given to increase our knowledge, but **to change our lives**. It will be important for you to study carefully the Scriptures given in this lesson to help you maintain a vibrant Christian walk as you travel life's road through to eternity.

KEY VERSE

Deuteronomy 8:3b *"...man does not live on bread alone, but on every word that comes from the mouth of God."*

I. THE IMPORTANCE OF GOD'S WORD

A. From the following Scriptures, give the importance of God's Word:

1. 2 Timothy 3:15 ____________________

S "We often take this verse to mean how the Bible will convict others when we quote it to them. It actually says that it will enable us to discern our motives."

2. Hebrews 4:12 ____________________

3. Psalm 119:9-11 ____________________

S "Throughout the ages, many attempts have been made to wipe the Bible off from the face of the earth, but it just keeps on spreading."

4. Matthew 24:35 ____________________

5. Acts 20:32 ____________________

6. Jeremiah 15:16 ______________________________

7. John 16:33 ______________________________

S "It seems that many of us forget to get comfort, help, or direction from the Word of God when everything is falling apart around us. Nevertheless, as you look back on your life, you may be able to see where the Word was a comfort and help for you as you proceed with the rest of the lesson."

B. Making the Word Practical

Choose a few of the above verses that have proven to be life-changing for you, and share it with the group.

II. THINGS THAT KEEP THE WORD FROM BEING EFFECTIVE IN OUR LIVES

A. Mark 4:19 describes three things that keep the Word from reproducing in our lives. What are they?

1. ______________________________

S "Worries can be divided into two categories:

- Self-produced. Which worries do you sense are self-produced?

- The result of living in a sinful world. Which are these?"

2. ______________________________

S "In what way is wealth deceitful? We think it will satisfy, but it will only make us wanting more."

3. ______________________________

S "In practical experience, how does this choke the Word?"

B. Share with the group where you have found victory to help you respond to the Word, or where you find it difficult because of the struggle with one or more hindrances mentioned in II-A.

T Listen for answers such as, "The concern over my ability to provide security, food, and shelter for my family", and "How I will be able to provide for my retirement".

III. EFFECTIVE WAYS TO HAVE GOD'S WORD TAKE ROOT IN OUR HEARTS

A. It takes discipline and time to make God's Word life-changing on a

daily basis. The following five Scriptures give you a guide to making God's Word a part of your daily life. Write these down.

1. Romans 10:17 ______________________________

S "This is why neglecting the Word is so harmful to us."

2. Revelation 1:3 ______________________________

3. 2 Timothy 2:15 ______________________________

T Emphasize that truth is not to be trifled with. It is the Living Word. God Himself is Truth.

4. Psalm 119:11 ______________________________

5. Joshua 1:8-9 ______________________________

S "In God's eyes, what would success look like a person's life?

CONCLUSION

You may not be able to begin to do all of the above in III, but you may choose one or two and commit yourself to beginning this week. For example, you may wish to begin reading the Word daily. Choose a book you will begin to read. Share your commitment with the group, and be prepared to share what you have learned.

T Suggest how they can make their reading and study of the Bible more meaningful by marking (underlining, highlighting, or writing notes) their Bible when they come to a spiritual principle which they think would be helpful to them. They will find that when certain trials come, they could turn to these Scripture portions for wisdom and guidance.

Next week, we will look at another very important aspect of growing to maturity as a Christian when we study the topic of **Freedom and Power Through Prayer.**

LESSON 11

FREEDOM AND POWER THROUGH PRAYER

S "Why is prayer necessary and important? Because it is the only means by which we can bind the power of Satan and unleash the power of God in our life. This is one of the child of God's most powerful weapons."

INTRODUCTION

For some time now, you have come to appreciate the fact that you have a personal relationship with God through Jesus Christ who lives in you by the Holy Spirit. However, God wants you to experience a deeper, more intimate relationship with Him.

Imagine you have a friend whom you deeply love. You want to spend time with him or her, but when you are in each other's company, you hardly ever talk or converse. That relationship would never deepen beyond what you observe about that person's appearance or actions. If, on the other hand, you begin to talk to the person, revealing your heart of love for him or her, you will begin to get a response. If then the person begins to communicate with you, the relationship is deepened in another dimension.

Prayer is intended to be a two-way conversation between you and God. As any communication between two people, you will discover that prayer has many levels of intimacy and trust as you learn to know God better. Freedom of expression and power to live the way God wants you to live will be the result.

This lesson will help deepen your insight into God's desire to equip you with what you need to overcome the enemy and be victorious in life.

KEY VERSES

Luke 11:9-10 *9 "So I say to you: Ask and it will be given to you; seek and you will find: knock and the door will be opened to you. 10For everyone who asks receives: he who seeks finds; and to him who knocks, the door will be opened."*

S "Persist in pursuing God. Knowing God takes faith, focus, and follow through. Jesus assures us that we will be rewarded."

1 John 3:21-22 *21Dear friends, if our hearts do not condemn us, we have confidence before God 22and receive from him anything we ask, because we obey his commands and do what pleases him.*

T You may wish to say the following before beginning to answer the questions:

"The Key Verses may put more questions in your mind about prayer than what they answer." Explain that God has conditions for answered prayer. Some of these will be covered in Section II of this lesson. You can also say to your students, "If we are truly seeking God's will, there are some requests you and I will not make. If we obey God, we will be asking in line with His will."

I. WHAT IS PRAYER?

Very simply stated, prayer is an intimate conversation—talking *and* listening to a personal God. One without the other is not conversation.

A. God Desires Conversation

1. What three significant words in our Key Verses, Luke 11:9-10, show us that God desires to have conversation with us?

________________ ________________ ________________

S "When you pray, remember that God is your heavenly Father and that He will do no less for His children than any earthly father can. And God is perfect—He can and will do so much more than imperfect, fallen people like us."

2. God desires to answer our prayers, but there is a condition. What is that condition? (1 John 3:21-22)

____

____

T At this point, do not seek an answer for the part of the verse that says, "you can ask anything and you will receive it". That will be answered to some extent in Section II.

B. Prayer: A Privilege and a Responsibility

We have many needs and great opposition from Satan who wants to hinder us in prayer and our pursuit of godliness. God wishes to meet our needs and the needs of others in a supernatural way. For this reason, you will discover many kinds of prayer. From the following prayers, tell what kind of prayer is being uttered.

1. Luke 18:13 – The publican or tax collector's prayer could be known as a prayer of... ?

____

S "This is a good example of immediate forgiveness as we come with a repentant heart recognizing our sinful state."

2. Matthew 26:41 – What reason do you see here for prayer?

S "Spiritual eagerness without the Spirit's power is often accompanied by carnal weakness. For example, Peter saying, 'I will die with Jesus'. A few hours later he denies Jesus."

3. James 5:16 – For what purpose is this kind of prayer?

S "Confession of sin and the prayer of faith bring healing, especially where sin is the cause of sickness."

4. What kind of prayer is Psalm 103:1-5?

S "Praising God is not for show—it needs to come from the heart."

List the things the psalmist is thankful for:

The study of prayer is a big and exciting subject which we cannot cover adequately here. As you read the Bible, watch for different kinds of prayer and try to model them and put them in your own words. To mention a few, there is **intercessory** prayer (for others); **thanksgiving** prayer for what God has done and is doing; and **petition** (praying for deliverance from sin and bondage). Trust God for whatever you truly need to be a more godly person.

II. DOES GOD ALWAYS ANSWER PRAYER?

The answer is, "Yes!" However, the answer is certainly not always as we desire, but is **always** what is best for us. Let us look at some possible answers.

S "Remember that God is perfect, and will do what is best for us."

A. What if the answer is "No"?

1. According to James 4:2-3, why is the answer sometimes "No"?

S "What examples can you think of?"

2. An example of a prayer that God would not answer is, "Lord, let me win the lottery ticket of 36 million dollars." Why do you think God would not answer this prayer?

T You may wish to share things you are praying for which you know are God's will. This will help them discern the motivation for that prayer request.

B. The answer may be "First, meet the conditions".

1. Psalm 66:18 tells us why God cannot answer certain prayers at the time we ask. What reason does He give?

2. What great results are there if we meet His conditions? (2 Chronicles 7:14)

T For discussion (if time permits): "What prayers do you believe we should pray for God to heal our land?"

C. The answer may be "Not yet".

The timing may not be right. God knows the end from the beginning. How is that made clear in the raising of Lazarus in John 11:1-14?

S "Jesus raised Lazarus from the dead (instead of preventing his death) so that Jesus would be glorified. Sometimes Jesus "delays" and has us wait until such a time as His name and His purposes will be more greatly magnified. It will be so evident that only God could bring it to pass. Also, it will ultimately be of most benefit to us in making us more like Jesus."

III. WHAT ARE THE BENEFITS AND RESULTS OF PRAYER?

There is often a radiance or a revealing air about a prayerful, faith-filled Christian. Let us discover what God promises to the suppliant or petitioner that brings this about.

A. John 16:24 – What result is promised?

____

S "Would anyone like to share an answered prayer?"

B. Acts 4:31 and Acts 1:8 – What result is there in answer to this prayer?

____

____

CONCLUSION

This is a good time to practice what you have learned about prayer. God asks us to be thankful. He has answered your prayer of repentance, for forgiving your sins; He has answered your prayer of coming into your life when you invited Him in. List some other prayers that God has answered, then list those prayers you know He would be pleased to answer.

PRAYERS HE HAS ANSWERED	PRAYERS HE WANTS TO ANSWER
1.	1.
2.	2.
3.	3.
4.	4.
5.	5.

Now, have a time of prayer of thanksgiving and petition (asking God). Pray in faith, believing and wait for the answer. Share the results in the coming weeks as you receive answers to your prayers.

LESSON 12

GOD, MONEY, THE CHURCH, AND THE CHRISTIAN

INTRODUCTION

Bringing up the topic of money in the Church is often as explosive as lighting a match in a room full of dynamite. You will hear remarks like, *"All they want is **my** money", "They are mixing the spiritual with the secular", "What I give is my business", "I can't afford to give; I have enough struggles trying to pay my bills", "If I hear the topic of money one more time, I'm leaving", etc.* This lesson will help you understand what relationship God, money, and the Church has to the Christian. Properly understood and used, money can be a great blessing to God's work and those who obey the principles God has set forth in the use of "worldly wealth".

S "Can you list other comments people make about the church and money? For instance, "Look how they are spending ***my*** money". (They do not realize that once they give something away it is no longer theirs to control)."

KEY VERSES

1 Chronicles 29:11-12 *[11]Yours, O Lord, is the greatness and the power and the glory and the majesty and the splendour, for everything in heaven and earth is yours. Yours, O Lord, is the kingdom; you are exalted as head over all. [12]Wealth and honor come from you; you are the ruler of all things. In your hands are strength and power to exalt and give strength to all.*

I. THE PRINCIPLE OF OWNERSHIP

A. Ownership of Our Bodies

1. On what basis can God claim ownership to our bodies? (1 Corinthians 6:19-20)

____

____

S "How are we violating this principle of God's ownership of our bodies in society today?" (For example, abortion, promiscuity, alcoholism, drug abuse, gambling)

2. Since our bodies belong to God, what responsibility would we have in regards to the use of our time for God? (2 Corinthians 5:15)

____

S "How do you think this would work out in our daily living—in our jobs, church, recreation, relationships, etc.?"

B. Ownership of Our Possessions

1. According to your Key Verses in verse 11, how vast is God's ownership?

____

____

S "What relationship do we have with our possessions? We are really only stewards of all we claim to own. How good are we as stewards of what is really God's property?"

2. Verse 12 of the Key Verses describes the source of wealth. What is it?

____

S "How much truth is there in boasting, 'I deserve this. I have earned it.'? Let us see what God's answer is in this next question."

3. You may say, "I have earned my money and deserve to use it as I please." What is God's answer in Deuteronomy 8:17-18?

____

____

4. According to Ecclesiastes 5:19, how should I view the enjoyment I receive from life as a result of my possessions?

____

____

II. THE PRINCIPLES OF ACCUMULATING WEALTH

A. There are wrong and bad reasons...

1. Luke 12:16-21 describes the motives of a certain rich man. What motives did Jesus judge harshly, and what were the consequences of using these motives to accumulate wealth?

____

2. There are wrong ways of accumulating wealth.

   a. What two principles about getting wealth do you see in Proverbs 13:11?

   b. Using these principles, where would purchasing lottery tickets fit in?

3. How is the wrong pursuit of riches a trap? (1 Timothy 6:9-10)

B. ...and there are right and good reasons.

Since wealth is a gift from God, it is also good. If used for what it has been designed, it can be of great blessing to the one who earns it and to the work for God. The Bible makes it clear that all of us are responsible to make money and to use it as designed. Let us look at some responsibilities we have toward God in regards to what we earn.

1. What does God see as our first responsibility of earned income? (1 Timothy 6:7-8)

2. It is well known that not everyone has the health or the mental capacity to earn his own way; however, God has set down some principles of providing for ourselves and others. What are they? (2 Thessalonians 3:6-14)

S "How should we view the huge salaries of athletes, actors, celebrities, etc. Should we desire these? Why or why not?" Discuss.

Note: Another motive for accumulating wealth taught in the Scriptures is that of giving for the purpose of helping the poor and the spreading of the gospel. In the next section we will be dealing with the principles and the blessing involved in using our financial resources for God.

III. GIVING: THE ULTIMATE BLESSING

God has demonstrated that giving is the ultimate blessing when He gave His Son (John 3:16). We will see how this gift keeps going on and on as we demonstrate our faithfulness in the principles of giving.

A. Considering the Principles for Giving

The Bible has given some clear guidelines for giving. See if you can list them from the following verses:

1. Deuteronomy 16:17 ________________________

2. 1 Corinthians 16:2 ________________________

3. 2 Corinthians 9:7 ________________________

4. 2 Corinthians 8:12 ________________________

S "What would you say to a person who says, 'If I won the lottery, I would give so much to the church or do this or that for a good cause?'"

B. Considering the Blessing of Giving

It is often said, "I just can't afford to give." The fact is that you cannot afford *not* to give when you consider the consequences of not giving and the blessing if you give. Consider Malachi 3:8-12.

1. What does God call the offense of not giving at least a tenth of the money that we earn?

____

____

2. What was the result of their not giving the tithe?

____

T Discuss: "Could it be that we live under a curse when we fail to give of that with which God has blessed us?"

3. Under what curse do you see we could be today, that may be a judgment of God upon us, in not being able to make our own way in providing for us and the family? (Malachi 3:9)

____

____

S "What other things may indicate a curse because of our unwise handling of money?"

4. God makes a promise of blessing to those who tithe (a tenth of their income). What could that be in today's economy? (v. 11)

____

____

T Elicit testimonies from those who have begun tithing.

5. Study Luke 6:38 and 2 Corinthians 9:6. Then, in your own words, describe the blessing received from giving.

____

____

C. To Whom Do I Give?

1. It is a good principle to give to the Church where you are being spiritually fed. This is called storehouse giving (Malachi 3:10). But there are other places to give, according to the Bible. What are they?

   a. Deuteronomy 15:7 ______________________________

   b. Acts 20:35 ______________________________

   c. 2 Corinthians 9:6-15 ______________________________

2. Paul describes how gifts to those who were spreading the Gospel were helpful in fulfilling the Great Commission. What other blessings come to those who serve through giving? (vv. 12-14)

____

____

3. What opportunities do we have today similar to what the givers did in Paul's day?

____

____

D. How Do I Give?

1. 2 Corinthians 9:7 ______________________________

2. Romans 12:8 __________________________________

CONCLUSION

When you consider the great blessings God has in store for those who give, what steps will you take in your life to put your finances on a biblical basis according to what you have learned today? Share this if you feel comfortable to do so.

ANSWER KEY

THIS IS MY NEW LIFE

INTRODUCTORY LESSON

II. YOU MAY HAVE PURSUED MANY PATHS THAT LEAD...

B. Your leader will guide you through this...

3. GROWING BY OBEYING

c. Obey....

i. **A person who builds a foundation by obeying the principles of God's Word when one hears them will be able to weather the storms of life when they come.**

ii. **What do you see as the result of not obeying what you hear? If we ignore or disobey the principles that we hear, we suffer loss. We will not be able to overcome the challenges of life.**

LESSON 1: FACING LIFE AS IT REALLY IS

I. FACING THE REALITY OF MY LIFE

A. Life as I Feel and See It

1. **[Answers will vary]**

B. Facing the Fact that I Am a Worshipper

2. **This verse says that every man instinctively knows there is "life" beyond the grave and/or they know there is a God whom they should worship.**

3. **[Answers will vary]**

4. **We are not able to figure out by ourselves God's actions and purposes from creation to eternity.**

5. **This passage also states that what seems right to godless people will lead them down the path to their own destruction. In other words, we do not have the ability to know God's ways and purposes within ourselves.**

C. God's Intended Life for Me

1. **God's original intent for us is to have all we need to enjoy life; to find fulfilment in our work and play, and in our service to others.**

2. **All that we have and enjoy is a gift from God.**

3. **Whatever God does lasts for eternity and cannot be improved upon. God has done this so man would honor (or revere) Him.**

LESSON 2: FACING MY SPIRITUAL...

I. HUMANITY AS ORIGINALLY CREATED BY GOD

A. God's Purpose for Creating Humanity

1. **He was made in the image of God to rule over the earth and its creatures.**
2. **This psalm states that we were crowned with glory (honor). Such is not spoken of concerning any other creature of God. Mankind is very special in the eyes of God. We were given responsibility to take care of the earth and its creatures.**
3. **Very simply stated, God's purpose for my life is to serve and worship Him. Only in this way will my life be fulfilled.**

B. Our Original Condition When God Created Us

1. **All that God had made was very good. In other words, perfect.**
2. **We were made in the image of God. We, as three-part beings, have body, soul, and spirit. God is Father, Son, and Holy Spirit. Like God, we are creative; we can think and love and feel like He does.**

II. OUR FALL FROM OUR ORIGINAL STATE

A. How Mankind Fell

1. **He questioned God, or made Eve question God.**
2. **Questioning God's motives; that He was trying to withhold something good from her.**
3. **She looked and saw, she desired, and then took the forbidden fruit, ate and shared it with Adam.**
4. **Our inner desire pulls us toward evil. This desire conceives and gives birth to sin. This sin has a child whose name is death.**

   Nugget: When we veer from God's way, we self-destruct.

5.
   a. **The responsibility is fully ours.**

   b. **We are fully to blame when we, by our own evil desires, choose to sin.**

B. The Result of Adam and Eve's Fall

6. a. **tried to cover their sin.**

b. **hid from God.**
c. **afraid of God; ashamed**
d. **blamed someone else for their sin**

7. a. **Increased pain in childbearing, desire will be toward her husband who would then rule over her.**

   b. **The ground was cursed, so he would have to work hard to make a living. It would produce weeds, and his food would come from the field that he would cultivate.**

CONCLUSION

Note: Do not try to teach your students at this point. Allow for expressions of feelings and their thinking about these subjects. The next lesson will deal with the truth which will confront them and the decision they will need to make when they understand and receive the truth about themselves and God's way for them to receive eternal life.

LESSON 3: ENTERING INTO MY NEW LIFE

I. QUALIFICATIONS FOR RECEIVING NEW LIFE

A. Repentance

1. **The Bible says that all of us have sinned. As a result we sin by doing our own thing. God includes all humans in the camp of sinners.**

2. **The Bible says that which God created displays his eternal power and divine nature, so that we are without excuse.**

3. **The Bible clearly teaches that unless we recognize that we are sinners, our souls will perish. Repentance is a necessary condition for becoming a citizen in the Kingdom of God, (Kingdom of Light).**

B. Giving Up Trusting in Ourselves

1. **All of our righteous acts are like filthy rags in God's sight.**

2. **The Bible tells us it is not through good works that we are saved, but according to His mercy. Our being saved will depend on what He has done for us (dying for our sin), and not what we can do for Him.**

C. Trusting in Jesus as Our Sin-Bearer

1. **He paid for our sins by dying on the cross for us. He took the**

punishment of our sins upon himself.

2. **He had to die a cruel death to pay the penalty of our sins.**
3. **We must receive Jesus into our lives.**
4. **The only way to heaven is through Jesus.**
5. **I must open my life to Him and ask Him to come into my heart to make me the kind of person that will obey Him.**

II. TAKING THE STEP TO RECEIVE NEW LIFE

Note: This is a very important section of this first manual. In your group, you will have people who are at various stages in their spiritual walk; those who have never been born again; those who have indicated in one way or another that they asked Jesus into their hearts; those who may be Christians and have no assurance of salvation; and those who know they are born again. Do not force the issue here, but encourage them to take this opportunity to seal their commitment to Jesus by praying this prayer with a group of people who will be delighted to help them as they begin their new walk with God. If you sense that an individual is not ready, say "You may wish to consider the cost of becoming a disciple of Jesus before you pray this prayer. It is very important that it is your decision, and that you are willing to first consider the cost of becoming a disciple of Jesus."

LESSON 4: KNOWING AND CLAIMING...

I. THE BASIS AND BENEFIT OF FORGIVEN SINS

A. The Basis on Which I Can Claim the...

1. **It is through Jesus, and only through Jesus, we receive the forgiveness of sins.**
2. **God will forgive the grossest and deepest sins if we meet his conditions. These are repentance, confession and by faith asking for forgiveness.**
3. **The blood of Jesus purifies us from all sin.**

B. Benefits of Forgiven Sins

1. **It will open our spiritual eyes to understand and to bring us from spiritual darkness to light. It releases us from the power of Satan.**
2. **His character of infinite grace in forgiving me all my sins.**
3. **Note: The recognition of God's grace upon our lives leads**

us to becoming gracious ourselves. See this develop in your disciples.

4. **I am a new person (a new creation). I am forgiven and God has cancelled my debt of sin that was against me. In other words, I can start over again.**

v.13 **I have been brought near by Jesus' shed blood.**

v.15 & 16 **He has made peace with me by being my peace.**

v.19 **I am now a fellow citizen of God's Kingdom and His people.**

v.21 & 22 **I now have become the temple wherein God lives.**

CONCLUSION

1. **If I have Jesus (the Son of God) in my life, I am a Christian.**
2. **The Spirit of Jesus (the Holy Spirit) within me confirms with my spirit that I am a Christian.**
3. **I must tell others that I have received Jesus into my life. This will give me further assurance that I am a child of God.**
4. **(Seek to get some commitments here).**

LESSON 5: RESPONSIBILITIES AND PRIVILEGES...

I. WHAT DOES THE BIBLE SAY ABOUT OUR...?

1. **Witnessing about the Gospel, if it is at all going to leave an impact, must be done in the power of the Holy Spirit.**
2. **Jesus visualized our witness to begin at home and gradually increasing our area of witness that would eventually reach the ends of the earth.**
3. **To go and make disciples (followers) of Jesus, baptizing them and teaching them to observe (obey) all things Jesus told us to obey.**

II. TWO EFFECTIVE TOOLS FOR PERSONAL EVANGELISM

A. The Witnessing Booklet

B. The Proper Use of the Personal Testimony

1. **You may also wish to emphasize that God's intention for them is to make their verbal testimony and godly life style a way of life for those who do not know Jesus.**
2. **Seek to give them examples from your life as to how they could write out each of a, b, and c.**

3. **Again, in this section you may have to give examples, because this may be very new to the majority of your class.**

4. a. **Give an example like: if the one to whom you will be witnessing seems to be bitter, angry, or fearful, try to illustrate an experience you have had with which they could identify.**

   b. **This need not be a long section, but should zero in on at least one area where God has effected change.**

   c. **Mentioning the positive aspects is very important. There will be enough doubt for the new Christian to handle without giving negatives that will be experienced by a new Christian.**

5. **Note: This is a key part of growth for a new Christian. Help them write out their testimony using the three essential elements:**

   a. **Have them use a few sentences stating the struggle in their life before they became a Christian.**

   b. **Have them state very clearly that they received or invited Jesus into their lives. Some may still say, "I always believed."**

   c. **Guide them into some ideas as to the change that has taken place. It is important that the emphasis should be more on the changes of their lifestyle than their feelings.**

TESTIMONY WORKSHEET

(For those who received Jesus as an adult)

Note # 1: To make the testimony easier to write, have them begin as it shows above, for example, "There was a time in my life..."

Note # 2: Demonstrate using From Darkness to Light, or the Four Spiritual Laws booklet, or Billy Graham's booklet, Steps to Peace With God, or some other tool to show them how they can use it with their friends to help them share their first testimony.

Note # 3 You will notice that the TESTIMONY WORKSHEET may not work for those who received Jesus as their Savior as a child. Refer those who received Jesus as a child to the next page for their outline.

LESSON 6: GROWING IN MY NEW LIFE AND...

I. OBEDIENCE: THE FIRST STEP TO BUILDING YOUR...

A. Following a New Master

1. **We must first hear the Word of God and then obey it in order to keep growing in our Christian walk.**

2. **If my life is grounded on the Word of God, when difficulties of life confront me, I will be able to keep my faith, and what's more important, be more solidly grounded and stable in my Christian walk when the storms are over.**

3. **Note: If there is some hesitancy here, be prepared to share the difficulty you have or are still facing. Your transparency will encourage others to share.**

B. Knowing the Foundation Upon Which to Build

1. **I must build upon the Foundation with integrity, dependence on God rather than wealth or fame; be rich in good deeds, rather than material wealth, and be generous and willing to share of what God has given me.**

2. a. **hearing**
   b. **reading**
   c. **memorizing (hiding it in our heart)**
   d. **meditating on the Word constantly**

II. WHAT DOES OBEDIENCE TO THE WORD DO FOR ME?

A. What do the following scriptures say the Word of God will do to transform us?

1. **Just as new babies desire milk, so we will grow spiritually when we take in the Word.**

2. **It judges the thoughts and attitudes of our hearts.**

3. **It is useful for teaching, rebuking, correcting, and training what is right; thus totally equipping the worker for Christian ministry.**

4. **Transform and renew our minds that will enable us to discern the will of God. (Before we were conformed to this world's ways and standards).**

5. **If the Word takes hold of our lives we will be cautious as to how we live. We will also become prosperous and successful.**

Note: If people hesitate to share, give them examples or share the greatest change that occurred in your life when you were saved.

III. THE SEARCH FOR INNER PEACE IS ENDED...

1. **God has clothed him with salvation (saved him) and given him a robe of righteousness. (God sees him as righteous, without blame.)**

2. **Not my joy, but the complete joy that Jesus has, will be in us.**

LESSON 7: THE HOLY SPIRIT: THE NEW LIFE...

I. THE HOLY SPIRIT IN RELATION TO THE BELIEVER

A. Study Romans 8:9

1. **The Holy Spirit lives within me.**
2. **Then we are not Christians or do not belong to Christ and our fleshly lusts control us instead of the Spirit guiding us.**

B. After reading John 14:16&17 explain

1. **The Holy Spirit is the Spirit of truth and the world or non-believer cannot understand or accept the Spirit of truth, nor do they understand the things of the Spirit.**
2. **We cannot expect the World or unbeliever to obey or even understand the laws of God. Those are understood only by those who have spiritual eyes.**

II. WHAT ROLE DOES THE HOLY SPIRIT HAVE IN THE...

A. According to your Key Verse, Ezekiel 36:27

1. **The function of the Holy Spirit is to enable us to want to obey God and His laws.**
2. **Note: Here you may wish to give an example from your life where you once were powerless and how Jesus helps you now in this area of your life.**

B. Romans 8:16 gives a very important function of...

1. **The Holy Spirit who is in us gives us the confirmation that we are Christians, i.e. only you know for sure.**
2. **You may want to suggest: a sense of peace; anger you once had is diminishing; people who once were your enemies are now your friends; a desire for the Word of God.**

C. How will the believer know the truth among...
Consider John 16:13

1. **Another name for the Holy Spirit is the Spirit of Truth, that is, He is Truth personified.**
2. **The Spirit of Truth will give me, as a believer, discernment as to what is true and what is false, as well as what I should do or not do.**

Now consider John 16:14.

3. **The Holy Spirit will help me to recognize that He will always glorify Jesus, not Himself. In the same way, someone who glorifies himself and not God is a false teacher or leader.**

A. What other role does the Holy Spirit have...

1. **The Holy Spirit will give us power to witness and speak for God, i.e. He takes away the fear of witnessing for Jesus.**
2. **He will teach us and remind us of those things we have heard, read and seen of spiritual truths. He helps us recall what we have learned.**
3. **He will bring conviction upon us and the world, about sin, what is right or wrong, and the judgment that will come as a result of disobedience.**
4. **It is our confession of our sin that breaks the barrier between me and God. When I have fellowship with God, I will also have fellowship with my fellow man.**

III. APPLICATION

Here you may have to review the basic principles of this lesson to give them an opportunity to understand what principles were most important for them.

You cannot force them to reveal these issues, but if an openness has developed in your class, some may be open to share.

LESSON 8: THE HOLY SPIRIT: RESIDENT OR...

I. BASIS UPON WHICH GOD CAN CLAIM OWNERSHIP...

A. God's View of Our Bodies

1. **He purchased us with His precious blood so He could take possession of our bodies (His temples) and use them for His glory.**
2. **Our life (body) is highly treasured because the Spirit of the living God indwells us, i.e. we are God's temple and our bodies are sacred. Therefore we dare not violate His standards for human life.**
3. **The one who destroys man (God's temple) God will destroy him.**

B. God's Reason for Owning and Possessing Our...

1. **Man without the Spirit does not want to nor can he obey God's laws. With the Spirit within us we can overcome the tempter's power and the power of the flesh which tends to destroy us.**
2. **You may wish to explain here that our problems are not solved when we become Christians. The battle with Satan has only begun, but our solutions are different and God's power is available.**

3. a. **carnal or unspiritual**

   b. **understand**

   c. **do not do; do**

   d. **is sin living**

   e. **nothing good lives**

4. a. **The first law is the law of sin. When I want to do good, evil wants to take over. This law also wages war with my mind and seeks to make me a prisoner.**

   b. **The second law is God's law. This law delights and wants to obey God's law by the power of the Holy Spirit.**

5. **The only answer for victory over those two laws at work to destroy him was Jesus Christ.**

6. **That power would come from the Spirit of Christ indwelling Him, as he gave Him control of his life.**

II. HOW CAN WE MAKE GOD, THE HOLY SPIRIT,...

A. What are God's conditions for us to be filled...

1. **He will give the Holy Spirit to them who obey Him, that is, His Word.**

2. **We must put to death (or surrender) whatever belongs to our sinful nature. These are sexual immorality, impurity, lust, evil desires, greed, anger, rage, malice, slander and filthy language, put off lying and all such things which defile the soul.**

B. How can I be filled with the Holy Spirit?

1. **This verse invites us to ask God to give us the Holy Spirit in full measure if we ask. If we do not ask, we cannot expect to receive.**

2. **Compassion, kindness, humility, gentleness, and patience, forgiving one another as the Lord has forgiven us.**

3. a. **He will enable us to claim His power to be His witnesses.**

   b. **We will manifest the fruit of the Spirit, which is love, joy, peace, patience, kindness, goodness, faithfulness, gentleness and self control.**

LESSON 9: WALKING IN THE SPIRIT THROUGH...

I. THE GREAT EXCHANGE PROGRAM

A. Keeping Short Accounts with God

1. a. **We still walk in darkness and lie and do not live by the truth.**

   b. **If we claim to be without sin, we are deceived and the truth is not in us.**

   c. **If we claim we have not sinned, we make God to be a liar and God's Word has no place in our lives.**

2. **He will forgive us our sins and purify us from all unrighteousness.**

3. **This will give us the transparency to have fellowship with one another and be an ongoing purification of our lives from sin.**

B. Jesus Is the Author of the Great Exchange...

1. From verse 1 what good news is Jesus to deliver?

   a. **That He will bind up the brokenhearted.**

   b. **He will free those captive to sin. (You could give the concept of captives to drugs and habits.)**

   c. **A release from darkness for those of us who were imprisoned in sin.**

2. Making the Good News of Jesus practical

   a. **Bind up the brokenhearted; draw near (or make His presence known to the brokenhearted). He will not despise a broken heart.**

   b. **Sin living in me. My sinful nature has no goodness of itself. Freed from that which bound me to sin and death.**

   c. **The truth of God and His Word will set us free.**

3. In Isaiah 61:3 we see three exchanges available to us. What are they?

   a. **a crown of beauty.**

   b. **the oil of gladness.**

   c. **a garment of praise.**

LESSON 10: SPIRITUAL HEALTH AND THE...

I. IMPORTANCE OF GOD'S WORD

A. From the following Scriptures give the...

1. **They are able to make us truly wise through putting our trust (faith) in Jesus Christ.**
2. **The Word of God enables us to judge our own thoughts and attitudes of our hearts. (It is not a sword to "cut" others with the Word of God, but helps us discern whether we are on the right way).**
3. **The Word keeps us from sinning if we hide the Word of God in our hearts.**
4. **Everything (material things) will pass away, but God's Word will remain.**
5. **God's Word of grace can build us up and give us an inheritance we share with those of like faith.**
6. **God's Word is the source of my joy and my godly desires.**
7. **God's Word gives us true peace and enables us to overcome the troubles this world hands us.**

B. Making the Word Practical

Note: You may wish to review all the things the Word does, in order to have them share the most important thing they sense God has done in their life.

I chose Hebrews 4:12. In life situations, whether it is opportunities or obstacles, the Word of God has enabled me to judge, to a great extent, the motives of my heart so that I would not take advantage of others or do only what I wanted to do. Our heart is very deceitful, and we can manipulate our thinking to fit what we want.

II. THINGS THAT KEEP THE WORD FROM BEING...

A. Mark 4:19 describes three things that keep the Word from reproducing in our lives. What are they?

1. **Worries of this life.**
2. **The deceitfulness of wealth which gives me a false sense that I can control my own destiny without God.**
3. **The desire to own "things" rather than to become more like Jesus.**

B. Share with the group where you have found...

In questions like this, you may wish to lead with an example from your own life. Your transparency will bring out transparency in others.

III. EFFECTIVE WAYS TO HAVE GOD'S WORD TAKE ...

A. It takes discipline and time to make God's...

1. **Hearing the Word leads to deeper faith.**
2. **We are blessed when we read, hear and obey the Word with our hearts.**
3. **We are to handle the Word of Truth correctly. (We sometimes use the Word to justify ourselves or try to change others to our own way of thinking.)**
4. **When I assimilate or keep in mind the Word, I will recognize sin when it approaches me, and I will be able to reject the temptation.**
5. **Meditating on the Word will enable us to do what it says. Success will then follow.**

CONCLUSION

Keep this assignment in mind for the next few lessons to encourage your group to read, study, and meditate on God's Word.

LESSON 11: FREEDOM AND POWER THROUGH...

I. WHAT IS PRAYER?

A. God Desires Communication

1. **Ask / Seek / Knock**
2. **If we have no unconfessed sin in our lives, our hearts will not condemn us, and thus we will be able to pray with confidence and in the will of God.**

B. Prayer: A Privilege and Responsibility

1. **Prayer of repentance or confession.**
2. **The Lord will keep us from falling into temptation as we pray and keep watch over our souls (lives).**
3. **Confessing sin to each other and then praying for each other, which leads to fellowship with one another.**
4. **This is a prayer of praise and thanksgiving.**

C. List the things for which the psalmist is thankful:

- **forgiveness of his sins**
- **healing of his diseases**

- **restoration of his ruined life**
- **the gifts of love and compassion**
- **the experience of complete satisfaction**
- **renewal of his inner being**

II. DOES GOD ALWAYS ANSWER PRAYER?

A. What if the answer is "No"?

1. **When we ask with wrong motives to spend the things we would receive for our own pleasure.**
2. **There are two reasons why this would be a prayer God did not need to answer. First, it is a form of gambling. Second, that money may not be good for me.**

B. The answer may be "First, meet the conditions."

1. **God cannot answer if I harbor (or cherish or keep) sin in my heart.**
2. **God will hear from heaven, will forgive our sin and bring healing to the situation (to our land).**

C. The Answer May Be "Not Yet."

Sometimes God waits until a time or situation arises that will most glorify His name and will be of most benefit to us in making us more like Jesus. By waiting to come to heal Lazarus, He demonstrated God's power to raise people from the dead.

III. WHAT ARE THE BENEFITS AND RESULTS OF PRAYER?

1. **When we ask, we will receive, resulting in joy that we could not otherwise experience.**
2. **This prayer, when prayed with a pure and earnest heart, brings the fulness of the Holy Spirit into our lives.**

CONCLUSION
Note: Keep this in mind to share how God answers their prayers. This is faith-building.

LESSON 12: GOD, MONEY, THE CHURCH...

I. THE PRINCIPLE OF OWNERSHIP

A. Ownership of Our Bodies

1. **In the first place, our body (temple) was received from God; and because we strayed away He bought us back with His own blood.**

2. **Since we belong to God we have an obligation to live for Him and to serve Him.**

B. Ownership of Our Possessions

1. **What He created belongs to Him. Therefore, everything belongs to Him.**

2. **All wealth and honor come from God.**

3. **It is really God who gives me the power and the strength to produce the wealth. I cannot boast about one thing.**

4. **We should see all blessings of wealth, health, family, etc. as gifts from God. Material things and eternal blessings should bring out a spirit of gratitude, and not pride, of what we have achieved.**

II. THE PRINCIPLE OF ACCUMULATING WEALTH

A. There Are Wrong and Bad Reasons...

1. **The motive of always wanting more, and at the same time taking God out of the picture and spending this wealth for his own pleasure, thinking he had a long time to live. That night God took his life and required of him accountability for his actions.**

2. a. **Dishonest money vanishes quickly, but money earned honestly little by little is of great profit.**

   b. **It would fit into fast money—with the motive of greed. Trying to get out of a tough spot in which we have cornered ourselves with unwise use of money.**

3. **We fall into temptation and many foolish and harmful desires that plunge us to ruin and destruction. Also, the love of money is the root of many evils. It can cause us to wander away from God and pierce us with much grief.**

B. ...and Right and Good Reasons

1. **The first responsibility is to earn our own way and not to depend on hand-outs from others. We need to be content if we have food and clothing.**

2. **Healthy people should not be idle; we should work for our own living if we are able. We need to make our disciplined work habits a model for others.**

III. GIVING: THE ULTIMATE BLESSING

a. Considering the Principles of Giving

1. **We need to give to God in the same proportion to what He has blessed us.**
2. **Giving should be regular, according to God's weekly blessings.**
3. **We should purpose in our heart to give with joy and not reluctantly.**
4. **It doesn't matter how little we have. God expects us to give of what we have.**

B. Considering the Blessings of Giving

1. **Robbing God of what belongs to Him.**
2. **Not giving to God what was rightfully His, brought them under a curse. As a result, their crops would be taken by pests, and their trees would cast their fruit.**
3. **It could be that our cars break down prematurely, and we could be loaded with all kinds of abnormal expenses.**
4. **He could prevent many things from happening that were mentioned in #3 and make our money go further in many ways.**
5. **The blessing I will receive will be according to what I give and with what spirit. The blessings will be many times greater than what I give.**

C. To whom do I give?

1. **Give to the poor.**
2. **Helping those who cannot help themselves.**
3. **Give to crises situations in our families, communities, country, and the world. For example, famines, earthquakes, etc.**

D. How do I give?

1. **cheerfully**
2. **generously**

CONCLUSION

Encourage students to share each other's blessings.